HOMEMADE DOG FOOD UNLEASHED:

Easy, Safe & Low-Cost Nutritious Recipes
to Revolutionize Your Canine's Diet for
Optimal Health, Wellness, and Vitality

TABLE OF CONTENTS

INTRODUCTION

Welcome to a journey that promises to fill your dog's bowl and enrich their life through the power of nutrition. This book is not just a collection of recipes; it's a testament to my journey. My love for cooking has always been a significant part of my life. However, it took on new meaning when I started preparing meals for my beloved Chihuahua, Dot. As you go through this book, you will discover how head over heels I am for my dog and what I am willing to do to improve her life and maintain its quality to the very end.

This book is born from that passion and the transformative experience of cooking for Dot, aiming to share that joy and empowerment with you. There's something magical about watching Dot scamper excitedly as I prepare her meals; she turns into a total wiggle-butt in eager anticipation of fresh homemade food. I'm sure many of you can relate to the joy of seeing your furry friend's excitement over a home-cooked meal. Think about how excited you get when you have a home-cooked meal! It is the same for your dog, if not more intense, mainly if you have been feeding kibble or dry food, maybe a little less with canned food, but yet, REAL food is many levels above the other options.

It all began when I whipped up a simple chicken and rice dish for Dot; she wasn't feeling well. Watching her devour this homemade meal with more excitement than she ever showed for her usual dog food was a turning point for me. I saw an opportunity to ensure she ate high-quality food and found joy in preparing it myself. At that moment, I decided to tap into my inner chef to craft meals that met Dot's dietary needs and suited her tastes. The results were more than I expected: Dot's energy levels soared. Although she's quite the couch potato, she used to bring some pong into the room, but that's no longer the case. As a white dog, Dot had brown tear stains under her eyes, which have now disappeared! This transformation in her health and vitality gave me hope and inspired me to share my journey with you.

And all those old wives' tales and admonitions about feeding your dog "people food"? Toss them out! Quickly! Yes, there are certain people foods you should NOT feed to your dogs. I will enumerate them as we go along. There are also certain people foods to avoid if your pup has specific dietary, allergic, or disease issues. We will cover them as well. But, most importantly, your dog can eat almost all the "good food" you should eat. And if you should avoid the food (potato chips, ice cream, fried chicken strips, etc.), you should avoid feeding your dog the food. It is just that simple. Good for you… It's probably good for them. But you will see me repeatedly remind you to check with your veterinarian first to be safe and sure.

The primary goal here is to demystify preparing homemade dog food. Whether you're a novice in the kitchen or an experienced chef like myself, this guide will make the journey enjoyable, accessible, and beneficial for your canine companion, regardless of their size or life stage.

This book stands out because it combines the rigor of AAFCO nutritional requirements with the creativity of home cooking. We'll explore budget-friendly ingredients and the importance of supplements, ensuring your dog gets all the nutrients it needs without breaking the bank. Each recipe in this book is carefully curated, balancing nutritional value with mouth-watering flavors your dog will love.

Many might think, "Isn't homemade dog food a bit over the top?" or "I've heard it's expensive and complicated." Let's put those myths to rest. This book will guide you through overcoming these challenges, proving that cooking for your dog can be a rewarding and straightforward part of your routine with some planning and knowledge.

A wonderful woman I know was shopping in the town's best boutique pet food store. She thought she was keeping her little pooch enrobed in the best food available… until the pooch had stomach and other issues. The vet required stringent diets, and the boutique store had those foods as well… deep into three figures a month. She heard people in her building talk about homemade dog food and learned what she could and couldn't feed her pooch. Net result: cut her dog food expense by 75%, feeding real food fresh food, and the dog has recovered (so far) nicely. It seems like she spends about two hours a week in prep. Aren't you willing to spend two hours a week to keep your pup healthy or help make him/her healthy again? Of course you are; you just need some direction and instruction…welcome to the book.

You'll learn about canine nutritional needs, selecting ingredients, meal preparation techniques, and how to customize meals for specific health concerns and life stages. This book is a comprehensive guide, walking you through every step of the process.

I also encourage you to connect with the broader community of dog owners embarking on this homemade dog food journey. Share your experiences, recipes, and tips on social media and online forums. A wealth of knowledge and support awaits this community, ready to help you navigate challenges and celebrate your successes.

As we embark on this journey together, I hope you feel inspired and confident in enhancing your dog's diet and overall well-being. With a sprinkle of love, a dash of dedication, and this guide, you're well on your way to becoming a gourmet chef for your canine companion. Let's make mealtime a highlight of their day, every day. Welcome to 'Homemade Dog Food Unleashed.'

How to use this book:

This book is a detailed cooking guide with helpful tips and techniques to ensure your fur baby receives optimal nutrition and variety. I created this book as a kitchen companion, inserting the tried and true time-saving methods I have learned from professional cooking after many years. Yes, being an experienced cook has helped me here, and now I can help you save time and money and understand the process and the reasoning. The primary cooking technique in this book is batch cooking, or what I like to call 'unleashed mode.' Combined with an easy-to-follow plan and highly customizable recipes that cater to your dog's specific health needs and conditions. With over 100 combinations, these easy-to-follow recipes offer helpful guidelines for preparing nutritious meals for your dog. No, you don't have to cook all 100 combinations; even 15 or 20 will be acceptable to get things going for quite a while as long as the pup likes what you are making.

Batch cooking means just what it sounds like. Make enough of one recipe for five or ten or more servings so you don't have to cook that recipe every two days. If you have six, eight, or ten good recipes stored away, you can go two to three weeks without having to cook again if the situation demands it. Of course, it is always better to be able to make a fresh meal in between the 'batches' whenever possible.

However, it is crucial to remember that you should use these recipes to supplement your dog's diet based on age, weight, and energy requirements. Seeking professional advice for feeding recommendations and determining the appropriate serving/portion size for your dog is not just advisable; it's essential for your dog's health and safety. Ultimately, deciding what to feed your dog is up to you. This book can be a valuable resource to help you make informed choices.

(Recipe Guidance: Most recipes are reduced to a small batch of food, as this is intentional; you want to start with small amounts to see if your dog likes the food first. If you get good feedback from your dog, you can go all-in on 'unleashed mode' just double or triple the ingredients for big-batch cooking results!)

Above all, remember to have fun! Don't hesitate to experiment, try new combinations, swap ingredients, and keep on learning. Like any skill, cooking requires practice.

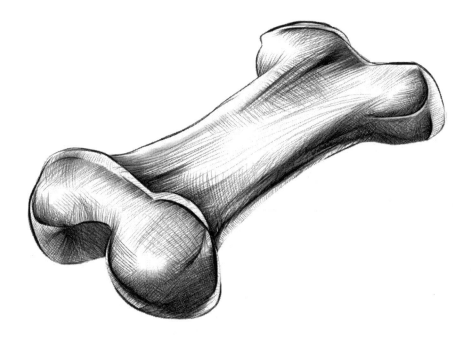

Chapter 1:

DEBUNKING THE MYTHS OF HOMEMADE DOG FOOD

One topic often discussed is whether homemade dog food is a good choice. However, many myths surrounding this topic make it difficult to know what to believe. This chapter aims to shed light on these myths and provide evidence-based insights for those who want to feed their dog's healthy meals made at home. So, if you want to learn more about what makes a balanced diet for your dog and how to prepare nutritious meals for them at home, this chapter is for you!

1.1 Myths About Homemade Dog Food

Nutritional Completeness Concerns

The myth that homemade dog food can't meet all of a dog's nutritional needs is pervasive yet unfounded. The truth lies not in the source of the food, commercial or homemade, but in the balance of nutrients it provides.

Achieving a nutritionally complete diet requires understanding the specific needs of dogs, which vary by size, breed, and life stage. For example, a balanced homemade meal for a dog might include a carefully measured blend of protein sources, vegetables rich in vitamins and minerals, a carbohydrate component for energy, and a fat source for essential fatty acids—all tailored to the dog's requirements. A vet or canine nutritionist can offer guidance, ensuring that meals provide everything necessary for a dog's health and vitality.

Expense Misconceptions

Another common misconception is that preparing homemade dog food is invariably more expensive than purchasing commercial diets. While it's true that buying premium or organic ingredients can be costly, savvy shopping can make homemade diets cost-effective. Consider a dog owner who buys bulk rice, vegetables, and meat, taking advantage of sales and seasonal produce. They manage costs efficiently by cooking in large batches and freezing portions while providing high-quality meals. The key is to plan and purchase smartly, considering the ingredients' price and nutritional value. We will cover many intelligent ways to do this at the end of the book.

As a second consideration, you can prepare meals for yourself as part of the program, reducing the overall cost even more. You might separate some ingredients and cook them yourself, with different add-ons, spices, and sauces, but chicken is chicken, and rice is rice. You eat it, and the pups eat it, too.

Time Demands

Many believe crafting meals for their dogs at home is a time-consuming endeavor that only those with ample free time can afford. Yet, this overlooks the efficiency achieved with some planning and knowledge. Preparing a week's worth of dog food can be as simple as setting aside a couple of hours one afternoon, much like meal prepping for any family member. The process can align with preparing the family's meals, utilizing the same fresh ingredients for convenience and nutritional alignment. For instance, while roasting vegetables for dinner, setting aside a portion to blend into a dog's meal prep requires minimal extra effort. Still, it pays off in quality and peace of mind. If you make similar meals for yourself, the time spent is even less since you are working on your meals simultaneously.

Safety and Health Fears

Safety concerns often deter pet owners from homemade diets fueled by myths surrounding the potential for nutritional imbalances and health risks. However, these risks diminish when owners educate themselves on dog-specific nutrition. Cooking at home allows for control over the quality and freshness of ingredients, a benefit seldom guaranteed by commercial dog foods. To dispel fears, consider the process of learning to cook for oneself—guided by research, advice from nutritionists, and a bit of trial and error, one develops the skill to create balanced, healthful meals. The same applies to preparing dog food; with the proper knowledge and approach, it becomes a safe, rewarding practice. Yes, indeed, it is no different than cooking for yourself.

The best preparation is a handy list of foods dogs should only sometimes eat. Then, with your vet, determine what foods your canine shouldn't have based on allergies, illnesses, and lack of compatibility. Check that list every time you make food for your pup.

1.2 Navigating Online Information: Reliable Sources

In today's world of endless information, knowing the best food to feed our dogs is essential. But with so much advice, it can take much work to understand what to trust. Some information can be helpful, while others can be confusing or misleading. So, the most important thing is to be careful about what we read and ensure it is reliable.

Identifying Credible Sources

When searching for reliable information about your dog's health and nutrition, it's essential to look for clues that indicate the information is trustworthy. Websites that cite professionals with veterinary or nutrition expertise and those that reference scientific studies are more likely to provide accurate information than those that rely on personal opinions or unverified claims. You can also look for credentials like degrees in veterinary medicine or affiliations with respected organizations to help you identify trustworthy sources. Articles that provide references and cite scientific research are precious because they allow you to learn more about the information and rely on solid evidence, not just someone's opinion. It would be good to ask your vet for places s/he would recommend for additional reading, including some of the places they research for information.

Expert Opinions

There is much conflicting information out there. But we can trust the advice of experts who have studied and worked with dogs for years. These experts know much about what dogs need to eat to stay healthy, and their guidance can help us make good choices. We can learn much by talking to these experts, reading their advice, and ensuring we do our best for our dogs.

Community Wisdom

In our modern world, there are many online communities and forums where people who own and love dogs can share information and advice about caring for them. These communities are beneficial because they have many different people with different experiences and perspectives. When someone asks a question, they can get many different answers that can help them figure out what to do. However, it's essential to be careful about the advice you follow and to only listen to people who know what they're talking about.

"Doing homework on your own can be difficult. Everyone sounds like an expert, but the real helper is likely someone from your vet's office if you can't sort out the static from the station."

When you're trying to learn how to feed your dog, there's a great deal of information out there, and it can be hard to know what to believe. But if you take the time to look for good sources of information and talk to experts, you can learn a great deal and ensure your dog is healthy and happy. Remember to be careful, curious, and prioritize your dog's well-being!

1.3 The Science of Dog Nutrition: What Research Says

Latest Findings

As we learn how to feed our dogs, researchers discover there's much to consider when preparing their meals at home. Recent studies by veterinary scientists show that dogs need a good balance of different protein types from animal and plant sources to stay healthy. By including a variety of proteins in their diet, we can ensure they get all the nutrients they need to keep their bodies working properly. It's essential to ensure our homemade dog food is nutritious and well-rounded! And may I repeat... this isn't very far from the advice given to us humans about our own dietary needs.

Nutritional Requirements

Recent studies have shown that dogs require certain nutrients to keep their muscles strong, their brain functioning well, and their coat healthy. Proteins are essential for muscle growth, especially for younger and active dogs. Fats provide energy and help with brain function and coat health, focusing on those rich in omega-3 fatty acids. Carbohydrates can provide essential dietary fiber and promote gut health, vital for your dog's overall health. If you are making homemade dog food, it's necessary to consider these factors and create a balanced diet that meets your dog's individual needs.

Supplementation Science

In the past, giving dietary supplements to dogs was based on guesswork and hearsay. However, scientific research has highlighted the importance of specific vitamins and minerals for canine health. For example, studies have shown that omega-3 fatty acids are good for joints and brain function when added to the diet of dogs with certain conditions. Similarly, probiotics promote good digestion by making the gut healthy. Following this scientific guidance, dog owners can ensure they're giving their pets the right supplements and not just guessing what might work. Again, checking in with your vet for this advice is highly recommended since some supplements in the wrong dosages can harm your four-legged friends, just as they can be dangerous to humans.

Debating Grain-Free

Grain-free dog food has become a debate among dog owners and nutritionists. Some studies have suggested that grain-free diets can help dogs with allergies and improve their coat health. However, there are also concerns about the risks of excluding grains from a dog's diet, such as an increased risk of heart disease. Pet owners must consider both the benefits and potential dangers of grain-free diets and choose based on their dog's needs and the latest research. Science can help guide us towards healthy and balanced food choices for our dogs, ensuring their diet is based on human trends and on what's best for their health and well-being.

1.4 Vet-Approved Advice: Incorporating Professional Guidance

Seeking Veterinary Input

Our relationship between pet owners and veterinarians is crucial in planning a balanced dog diet. Consulting a veterinarian is not just a formality but an essential step toward ensuring that homemade meals provide sustenance and nourishment. The veterinarian's expertise in animal physiology and nutritional science enables a personalized approach to diet formulation, which considers each dog's unique requirements, such as age, breed, activity level, and existing health conditions. This collaboration ensures each meal provides the necessary nutrients for optimal health.

Nutritional Assessments

When making homemade food for your dog, ensuring they get all the nutrients they need to stay healthy is crucial. That's where a nutritional assessment comes in. A veterinarian can evaluate the diet you plan to make for your dog and confirm it has everything they need in the right amounts, and help prevent health problems from developing in the future. Think of it like a sculptor making sure every detail of their creation is just right - the veterinarian fine-tunes the recipe. Hence, your dog gets the perfect balance of nutrients. By doing this, you can ensure, as much as possible, that your dog is healthy and happy for years. Make mote to keep within previously held ranges for proteins, fats, and carbs when making changes. Getting out of balance can create as many problems as you are trying to solve.

Addressing Health Concerns

Like humans, dogs can have health problems like diabetes, kidney issues, or being overweight. It's important to plan their diet carefully. Vets can advise us on changing their diet to keep them healthy and avoid diseases. We can help our dogs live longer, healthier lives by adjusting their food intake, choosing ingredients that won't raise their blood sugar too much, and ensuring they get enough nutrients to keep their kidneys healthy. Good nutrition is vital for dogs, especially when dealing with health problems.

Weight is often the most common and easiest to resolve. Slight cutbacks from 16 ounces of food to 12 ounces every other day is the same as cutting out one 16-ounce feeding every week. If that holds true for your pup, then within a month, they should be down a few percentage points of weight. By keeping track, you can discover that a few months down the road, you have achieved the vet's desired weight for your pup without any drastic diets or changes. Of course, if your dog is substantially overweight, more needs to be done, and consulting the vet is the course of action. Likely, s/he will say to cut food back four ounces daily instead of every other day. Hopefully, it can be this simple.

Preventive Nutrition

Taking care of our dogs before they get sick is becoming a popular way to feed them. Experts in animal health suggest adding certain nutrients to homemade food to help our dogs stay healthy now and in the future. Nutrients include antioxidants to help fight diseases, omega-3 fatty acids to help with brain function and joint health, and fiber to help with digestion. Using their knowledge of what nutrients our dogs need, veterinarians can help us ensure they get the right food to keep them healthy.

1.5 Educational Resources for Continued Learning

It's essential to know how to feed our dogs in a way that keeps them healthy and happy. Luckily, many resources are available to help us learn how to make nutritious meals for our dogs. However, understanding the world of canine nutrition can be complex and ever-changing. That's why it's essential to keep learning and engaging with a community of experts and fellow pet owners who share the same goal: ensuring our dogs are healthy and happy.

Books and Publications

We want to make sure they are getting the best nutrition possible. There are many books on the subject, but it's essential to choose ones written by experts in animal health and nutrition. It is also important to note the copyright year on the inside front page. If it is current, then the information should be current. If it is older, over five years, then unless it is considered a 'classic dog food book,' you should strongly consider newer titles. These books provide helpful information, like real-life examples, different nutritional theories, and tips on feeding your dog based on age and health condition. If you're starting, it's also helpful to read books that explain how diet affects the body and overall health of dogs.

Online Courses and Webinars

With the advent of digital education platforms, access to structured learning experiences, once the purview of professional training programs, has expanded into the public domain. Universities and professional organizations frequently host webinars and online courses, often at minimal or no cost, led by experts in veterinary nutrition and canine care. These sessions impart theoretical knowledge and offer practical demonstrations of meal preparation, dietary assessment, and nutritional optimization for dogs with specific needs. Engaging in these courses facilitates a bridge between foundational knowledge and its application, enabling pet owners to tailor dietary plans with confidence and precision. This is one of the better ways to learn since the people running the programs are considered experts, the information they provide is new and expert-level, and the results and trends are current for dogs and dog owners alike.

Workshops and Seminars

If you prefer to learn by doing things with your hands, workshops and seminars are a great way to gain practical experience. These events are usually led by nutrition and animal healthcare experts, giving you guidance and support. These events, whether held in physical venues or through virtual platforms, present opportunities for direct interaction with instructors, fostering an environment where questions and discussions deepen the understanding of canine dietary needs. Participating in cooking demonstrations, nutritional planning sessions, and health assessment workshops imbues pet owners with the skills necessary to navigate the complexities of canine nutrition, transforming abstract concepts into tangible practices. The cooking demonstrations are most valuable for beginners, providing the much-needed push into the kitchen, knowing things will be fine.

Continual Learning

With so many different opinions and information, it can take time to understand what's best. Luckily, many ways to learn about dog nutrition can help you make informed decisions. To stay up-to-date on the latest research and trends in dog food planning, you can read articles, utilize the resources and references at the back of this book, follow trusted blogs, and join groups focused on dog health. By staying informed, you can ensure your dog gets the best food possible, which can help them stay healthy and happy.

Remember, you're not alone on this journey – many other dog owners are on it too! Together, we can ensure our dogs get the best care and nutrition possible. So, let's keep learning and applying what we know to care for our beloved pets in the best way possible.

One final note here: Do not drive yourself crazy over this. Focus on five or ten meals, get your information in order, make sure the foods are good for your pet, and then start cooking. Trying to keep a year's worth of information in your head will make it explode and won't help your pup.

Chapter 2:

PROTEINS, FATS, AND CARBOHYDRATES

Proteins are essential for keeping dogs healthy and robust. They are building blocks that help dogs' bodies grow and repair muscles, make hormones, and fight off sickness. However, not all proteins are the same. Some proteins are better than others, depending on where they come from and how easy they are for dogs to digest. Proteins from animal sources like chicken, beef, or fish are better for dogs than those from plants because they have all the essential pieces that dogs need.

The best protein sources for dogs should be highly digestible, of high biological value, and suitable for the dog's age, size, and health status. Here's a list of some of the best protein sources for dogs:

Meats
- **Chicken:** Lean, easily digestible, and rich in essential amino acids. It's a common ingredient in dog foods.

- **Beef:** Offers high-quality protein and is a good source of iron, zinc, selenium, and vitamins B12 and B6.

- **Turkey:** Another lean meat that is low in fat and easily digestible for most dogs.

- **Lamb:** Often used in dog food for pets with food sensitivities or allergies to other meat proteins.

Fish

- **Salmon:** Rich in omega-3 fatty acids, which can promote skin and coat health. Ensure salmon is well cooked to avoid parasites. Chef note: Canned salmon is a high-calcium option if you can't source fresh/frozen.

- **Sardines** are small fish that can be fed whole, including bones, for calcium and other minerals. Compared to larger fish, they are low in mercury. Chef note: Many kinds of products related to sardines are on the shelf. One of my favorites is Season brand Sardines in water, with no salt added. As with people, water instead of oil and no salt added are good points for our pups.

- **Whitefish:** Typically low in fat and calories, making it a good option for weight management. Whiting, Haddock, Herring, Hake, Pollock, Grouper, Catfish, Snapper, and Perch.

- **Fish to Avoid:** Certain fish, including bottom feeders and certain white fish, such as king mackerel, swordfish, tuna, eels, sea bass, lake bass, trout, flounder, and cod, contain high mercury or toxins. These can cause nervous system issues in dogs and take months to leave their system. The only way to utilize these fish would be if they were farmed instead of wild-caught.

Eggs & Dairy

- **Whole Eggs** are highly digestible and one of the most complete sources of amino acids. They are also rich in vitamins and minerals.

- **Cottage Cheese** is a source of lower lactose protein, making it easier for dogs to digest. It's also a good source of calcium.

- **Yogurt:** Can be a good source of protein and probiotics, but choose plain, unsweetened varieties and only in small quantities to avoid digestive upset.

Plant-based Proteins

- **Quinoa** is a complete protein containing all essential amino acids. It's also gluten-free and rich in fiber, and many people likely keep it in their food pantries.

- **Black Beans:** The chef recommends this, which is my favorite! It has it all—a no-grain superfood packed with protein, amino acids, and fiber! You can't go wrong with this one! Be careful not to overfeed; too much plant fiber can lead to intestinal gas issues. Translated... don't let Fido attend your fancy dinner party after eating a bowl of black beans.

- **Lentils and Chickpeas** are good plant-based protein, fiber, and micronutrient sources. They may require a few extra minutes of prep time, but they are well worth it.

Organ Meats

Organ meats, or offal, are highly nutritious and can be a valuable part of your dog's diet. They are typically rich in vitamins, minerals, and essential fatty acids. If using these organs makes you nervous, then feel free to cook them to ensure they are edible and safe. This should put your mind and nervousness at ease. Here is a list of organ meats that are both safe and nutritious for dogs, focusing on those that are generally easier to find:

Liver

- **Why It's Good:** The liver is a powerhouse of nutrition, packed with vitamins A, D, E, K, and B, as well as minerals such as iron and copper. It's also one of the most commonly available organ meats.

- **Caution:** Feed in moderation to avoid toxicity due to its high vitamin A content.

Kidneys

- **Why It's Good:** Kidneys are a good source of vitamins like B12 and minerals such as selenium, iron, and zinc. They can support kidney health and are generally well-tolerated by dogs.

- **Preparation:** They should be cleaned and cooked before feeding to remove impurities.

Heart

- **Why It's Good:** The heart is rich in taurine, an essential amino acid for dogs, which supports heart health. It's also a good source of protein and B vitamins.

- **Preparation:** It can be fed raw or lightly cooked, depending on your dog's diet and health status.

Spleen

- **Why It's Good:** Though not as commonly used as other organ meats, the spleen is a good source of iron and protein.

- **Preparation:** Like other organs, meats need to be cleaned and can be served raw or cooked.

Lungs

- **Why It's Good:** Lungs are a lower-calorie option that is high in protein and provides a good vitamin C source.

- **Usage:** Lungs are often a dehydrated form as a treat rather than a main dietary component.

General Tips and Guidelines on Organ Meats:

- **Variety and Balance:** Offer a variety of organ meats to provide a range of nutrients. However, due to their high nutrient content, organ meats should not make up more than 10% to 15% of the dog's diet.

- **Introduction:** Gradually introduce any new food, including organ meats, to avoid gastrointestinal upset.

- **Source Quality:** Choose organ meats from reputable sources to ensure they are free from hormones, antibiotics, and contaminants. Organic meat sources would be beneficial in this instance.

- **Cooking and Preparation:** Cook meats to kill harmful pathogens and avoid feeding seasoned or processed meats that contain harmful additives or high levels of salt.

- **Consultation:** Always consult with a veterinarian or a canine nutrition specialist, especially for dogs with specific health concerns or dietary needs or when introducing new foods.

Sourcing high-quality organ meats and other ingredients for your dog's diet requires research and vigilance, mainly if you aim for the best nutritional value and safety. Here's where and how you can source the organ meats mentioned:

Butchers and Meat Markets

- **What You Can Find:** Fresh liver, kidneys, heart, spleen, and lungs from various animals (beef, chicken, lamb, etc.).

- **Benefits:** High-quality, fresh organ meat is often available. Some butchers can provide specific cuts on request or advise on the best options for dog consumption.

- **Tips:** Build a relationship with your butcher; they can be a valuable resource for sourcing the best and freshest ingredients. If you let them know what is on your list, they can hold specific items for you for a day or so (you want them to be fresh).

Farmers' Markets

- **What You Can Find:** Locally sourced, organic organ meats are fresh and nutrient-dense. Again, the key here is organic, which is a significant benefit and worth more to buy.

- **Benefits:** Buying from local farmers is a good choice. You can get healthier options like grass-fed and free-range products, which are more natural and contain fewer chemicals or hormones.

- **Tips:** Talk to the farmers about their animal raising and feeding practices to ensure you get the highest quality.

Specialty Pet Stores

- **What You Can Find:** Dehydrated or freeze-dried organ meats like lungs, liver, and heart, often packaged as treats.
- **Benefits:** Convenient and often sourced from quality ingredients, these are easy to store and serve.
- **Tips:** Look for products with no added preservatives or chemicals. Single-ingredient treats are best.

Online Retailers

- **What You Can Find:** There is a wide range of options, including raw, freeze-dried, and frozen organ meats from various animals.
- **Benefits:** Getting your stuff delivered to your doorstep is super convenient. Plus, shopping in bulk can save you some extra bucks!
- **Tips:** Research the brands and read product reviews to ensure quality. Look for suppliers who use responsibly raised animals. However, this will be more difficult research than going to the butcher or the farmer's market.

Ethnic Supermarkets

- **Types:** Some organ meats, such as spleen or certain types of liver and kidneys, may be rare in regular supermarkets.
- **Benefits:** Ethnic markets often have a broader selection of organ meats at competitive prices.
- **Tips:** Familiarize yourself with the store's sourcing and handling practices to ensure quality and safety.

By sourcing the best ingredients for your dog, you're investing in its health and well-being. Always consult with a veterinarian or a qualified pet nutritionist when making significant changes to your pet's diet to ensure it meets its nutritional needs.

Energy Sources

The canine nutrition narrative is incomplete without fats and carbohydrates, each contributing uniquely to the energy matrix. Fats, dense in calories, offer more than just energy; they are essential for absorbing fat-soluble vitamins (A, D, E, and K) and maintaining the integrity of a dog's skin and coat. The type of fat matters significantly, with a preference for sources rich in omega-3 and omega-6 fatty acids, known for their anti-inflammatory properties.

Carbohydrates, often viewed through skepticism, hold value when included judiciously in a dog's diet. Thanks to their rapid conversion into glucose, they provide a quick energy source. Beyond energy, carbohydrates contribute to dietary fiber, promoting digestive health and facilitating bowel regularity. The choice of carbohydrates is crucial, with a nod towards complex carbohydrates like sweet potatoes or barley, which offer sustained energy release and essential nutrients. Just as with us, too many carbs is not a good thing either for the furries.

Each fruit listed can offer different benefits to dogs when fed in appropriate amounts and prepared correctly. Here are some benefits associated with fruit:

- Apples are a great source of fiber and vitamins A and C. Remember to remove the seeds and core, as seeds contain cyanide.

- Bananas are nutritious snacks packed with vitamins, fiber, biotin, copper, and potassium. They are low in cholesterol and sodium but high in natural sugars.

- Blueberries have antioxidants, fiber, and vitamins C and K. They can help boost a dog's immune system and improve skin health.

- **Cantaloupe:** This fruit is rich in vitamins A, B6, and C, plus fiber, niacin, folate, and potassium. It's also hydrating but high in sugar, so serve it in moderation.

- **Cranberries:** Cranberries are good for urinary tract health and can prevent bacteria from adhering to the walls of the urinary tract. Give them in small quantities, as too many can upset your dog's stomach.

- **Mango:** This fruit contains vitamins A, B6, C, and E, along with potassium, beta-carotene, and alpha-carotene. However, the pit is a choking hazard, so remove it before giving it to your dog.

- Oranges are a great source of vitamin C, potassium, and fiber. Remove the peel and use the fleshy part.

- Peaches are a good source of vitamin A and fiber, which can help fight infections and improve gut health. However, the pit contains cyanide.

- Pears offer vitamins C and K, fiber, and copper. They benefit the dog's colon health but remember to remove the seeds and core.

- **Pineapple:** This fruit contains bromelain, an enzyme that helps dogs absorb proteins. It's also high in vitamins, minerals, and fiber.

- Strawberries are a great source of fiber and vitamin C; their enzymes can also help whiten your dog's teeth as they eat them.

- **Watermelon:** Made of 92% water, it's a great hydration snack. It's also packed with vitamins A, B6, C, and potassium. Remove all seeds and the rind to prevent intestinal blockage.

2.1 How much to feed our dogs, putting it all together

Canine nutrition lies in balancing these macronutrients; the ideal ratio of proteins, fats, and carbohydrates does not subscribe to a one-size-fits-all philosophy. Many factors include the dog's life stage, activity level, and any specific health concerns. For instance, a highly active working dog has elevated energy requirements, necessitating a diet richer in fats and proteins to sustain their vigor. Dogs with a slower metabolism and less active lifestyle can benefit from a diet that is lower in calories. However, it should also contain high-quality proteins. Proteins maintain muscle mass without causing excessive weight gain.

The right balance of homemade dog food ensures your dog gets all the necessary nutrients. However, the perfect balance can differ for each dog, depending on age, size, breed, activity level, and health problems. Some general guidelines exist, but getting different opinions is also okay.

You should start by feeding your dog 2-3% of its body weight daily. For instance, if you have a healthy 50-pound dog, you can use this as a guideline. Additionally, it's important to know that a cup of fresh homemade dog food typically weighs around 8 ounces, which can be helpful to remember when preparing meals for your pup.

Steps:

- Calculate the daily food weight:
    - 2% of 50 lbs.: (50 * 0.02 = 1lb.)
    - 3% of 50 lbs.: (50 * 0.03 = 1.5lbs.)
- Convert pounds to ounces:
    - 1 lb.: (1 * 16 = 16oz)
    - 1.5 lbs.: (1.5 * 16 = 24oz)
- Convert ounces to cups (for fresh homemade food):
    - With the approximation that 1 cup of fresh homemade dog food weighs about 8 ounces:
    - 16 oz:(16 \ 8 = 2 cups)
    - 24 oz:(24 \ 8 = 3 cups)

Summary

- Daily food amount (weight): 1 to 1.5 pounds
- Daily food amount (ounces): 16 to 24 ounces
- Daily food amount (cups of fresh homemade food): 2 to 3 cups

Identifying if Your Dog is Receiving the Right Amount of Food

Overfeeding can lead to health concerns like obesity, significantly impacting your dog's health and quality of life. Conversely, underfeeding can result in malnutrition, which can also have serious health consequences. One simple way to check if your dog is at a healthy weight is by visually assessing its body condition, particularly focusing on its ribs.

The Rib Test

1. To properly assess your dog's weight, stand directly above it and look down while your dog is standing straight up. This will give you a clear view of the body alignment and help you assess the weight accurately.

2. Run your hands along their sides, feeling for their ribs.

3. They are likely overweight if you can't feel your dog's ribs without applying pressure. Not being able to see or feel the rib bones indicates you may need to reduce the amount of food or increase exercise.

4. If you can see more than the last two ribs, your dog may be underweight. In this case, you may need to increase their food portions or consult a veterinarian to rule out any underlying health issues.

Ideal Body Condition

In a dog with an ideal body condition, you should be able to feel their ribs with gentle pressure, but they should not be visibly protruding. Additionally, your dog should have a visible waist behind their ribs when viewed from above. From the side, their abdomen should tuck up slightly from their ribcage to their hind legs.

Every dog is unique, and their nutritional needs may vary. Seek professional advice if you need clarification about your dog's body condition or dietary requirements.

Overweight	Ideal Weight	Underweight

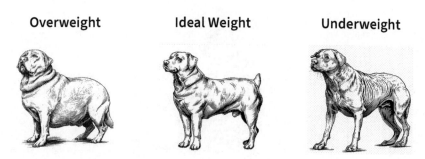

Basic Nutritional Components

- **Protein:** Proteins are crucial for muscle and tissue repair and growth.

Sources can include cooked lean meats like chicken, turkey, beef, pork, and fish. Eggs and some legumes can also be good protein sources. Typically, protein should make up about 18-25% of the diet for adult dogs and up to 29% for puppies, though this can vary. Some raw food enthusiasts suggest upward of 50% - 80%. This may be going a bit overboard, so consider all expert advice before deciding.

- **Fats:** Fats provide energy, help absorb specific vitamins, and support skin and coat health. Sources include oils like fish oil, flaxseed oil, and coconut oil, as well as fats from meats. Fats should comprise about 10-15% of the diet.

- **Carbohydrates:** While dogs don't have a strict dietary requirement for carbohydrates, they can be an essential energy source and provide fiber for digestive health. Whole grains like brown rice, barley, oats, and vegetables can be good sources. Carbohydrates vary widely in the diet, from 30% to 70%, depending on the dog's energy needs. Keeping the percentage around 45-55%.

- **Vitamins and Minerals:** These help maintain good health. Our dog's diet should include various vitamins and minerals that support the bones and immune system. Dogs can get these nutrients by eating multiple fruits and dark green veggies.

BALANCING THE BOWL

FATS (15%)

Coconut oil, olive oil, peanut butter, etc.

PROTEIN (25%)

Fish, beef, turkey, black beans, chicken, etc.

CARBOHYDRATES, FRUITS, AND VEGGIES (60%)

Rice, sweet potatoes, carrots, green beans, broccoli, apples, berries, etc.

A balanced diet is essential to your dog's health. This book strives to provide recipes that carefully balance fats, protein, carbohydrates, fruits, and veggies.

Life Stage Consideration

Dogs can have different nutritional needs based on their age and activity level. Puppies require higher protein and fat levels, while adults need a well-rounded diet. Senior dogs may need special diets to manage chronic health issues. Choosing the right food for your dog improves health and vitality. With knowledge about its dietary needs, you can craft a diet that enhances well-being and deepens your bond.

2.2 Vitamins, Minerals, and Supplements

While natural food sources like lean meats, fish, and vegetables are ideal, sometimes supplements can help. However, you should consult a vet before choosing any supplement for your dog, as they can guide you on reputable brands and dosages tailored to your dog's needs. Deficiencies or excesses of specific nutrients can lead to health issues. Be aware of the signs and adjust your dog's diet accordingly. Supplements are necessary to address nutritional gaps and particular health needs that a regular diet may miss. Choosing the right supplement can be complex, and it's essential to consider quality, necessity, and whether to go for natural or synthetic versions. Your vet can help you decide which supplement suits your dog's needs. Sometimes, dogs need supplements at certain life stages, health conditions, or if they are athletic. Too much supplementation can be harmful, so always stick to the recommended dosages. When used correctly, supplements can enhance your dog's health and vitality.

2.3 Raw Food Guidelines - Beginner's Guide to Preparing Raw Meals for Your Dog

Raw food diets have gained popularity among dog owners who believe feeding their pets a diet similar to what they would eat in the wild can improve health, better digestion, and a shinier coat. The benefits of such diets, including the natural adaptation of dogs to raw meat and bones, are encouraging and can motivate dog owners to explore this dietary option. However, it's important to note that preparing raw food for your dog requires careful planning and adherence to specific guidelines to ensure your pet receives all the necessary nutrients while minimizing the risk of foodborne illnesses.

Dogs have a unique digestive system specially adapted for raw meat and bones. This unique adaptation results from several key factors that pet owners should understand.

Dogs have a highly acidic stomach environment, with a pH of 1-2, especially when digesting raw meat. This acidity effectively neutralizes harmful bacteria and aids in bone digestion. The canine digestive system is also relatively compact, allowing food to pass through quickly, limiting bacterial growth, and reducing the risk of infections. This rapid transit is especially beneficial for processing raw meat and bones.

As descendants of wolves, dogs have a natural affinity for raw meat. Their digestive systems are equipped with specific enzymes for breaking down animal proteins and fats, and their immune systems are adept at handling potential pathogens in raw food. In the wild, canines consume entire prey animals, including meat, organs, and bones. This natural adaptability reassures dog owners about the suitability of raw diets for their pets.

Although dogs are naturally equipped to handle raw diets, it's crucial to implement them responsibly. This involves ensuring food quality and safety, selecting appropriate bones, maintaining balanced nutrition, and seeking veterinary consultation before transitioning. Understanding these factors helps explain dogs' ability to safely consume raw meat and bones. It empowers you to implement a responsible raw diet for your pet. Notably, considerably greater caution must be exercised when purchasing, handling, cooking, and serving food to your pups.

Additionally, their initial reactions to the new foods should be paid close attention to, as the raw aspect may influence these. Lastly, as with all 'current trends,' it's essential to recognize that this may change as more research is conducted. Keep an eye out for signs of nutrient deficiencies, such as dull coat, weight loss, or digestive issues, which may indicate that your dog's raw food diet is not providing all the necessary nutrients.

The Basics of Raw Feeding

A raw food diet for dogs typically consists of the following components:

- **Muscle meat:** This should comprise approximately 70-80% of the diet and can include chicken, beef, turkey, lamb, or game meats.

- **Organ meat:** Approximately 10% of the diet should consist of organ meats such as liver, kidney, or heart, as they are rich in essential nutrients.

- **Bone:** Raw bones, such as turkey necks or chicken and beef bones, should comprise about 10% of the diet. They provide calcium and other minerals. Using raw bones is crucial, as cooked bones can splinter and cause choking or internal injuries. Watch the raw bones as well for potential problems.

- **Vegetables and fruits:** For added nutrients and fiber, a small portion of the diet (around 5-10%) can include non-starchy vegetables and fruits such as leafy greens, carrots, and berries.

Tips for Preparing Raw Food

- **Source high-quality ingredients:** When possible, choose human-grade, fresh meats and organic produce to ensure the highest quality nutrition for your dog.

- **Practice proper food safety:** Always wash your hands, utensils, and surfaces thoroughly when handling raw meat to prevent cross-contamination and the spread of bacteria.

- **Balance the diet:** Consult a veterinary nutritionist to ensure your dog's raw food diet is balanced and meets all their nutritional needs. This is especially important for puppies, senior dogs, and those with health conditions.

- **Introduce raw food gradually:** When transitioning your dog to a raw food diet, gradually over 7-10 days to allow their digestive system to adjust and minimize the risk of gastrointestinal upset.

- **Monitor your dog's health:** When feeding a raw diet, monitor your dog's weight, energy levels, and stool quality closely. Consult your veterinarian if you notice any concerning changes.

Insights and Precautions

- **Not all dogs are suitable for raw feeding:** Some dogs with compromised immune systems, certain health conditions, or those in households with young children immunocompromised individuals may not be good candidates for raw diets due to the increased risk of bacterial contamination.

- **Proper storage is essential:** Raw food should be stored in the refrigerator or freezer and thawed in the fridge before serving to minimize bacterial growth, such as salmonella in raw chicken.

- **Avoid feeding raw diets in public spaces:** To reduce the risk of spreading bacteria to other dogs or people, avoid feeding your dog raw food in public areas such as dog parks or on walks.

Please consider the following when feeding your dog 80% meat(s):

One common mistake people make when feeding a home-cooked raw diet is forgetting to add calcium. Calcium is a crucial mineral for your dog's health, as it acts as a phosphorus binder, preventing high phosphorus levels that can be dangerous. Adding calcium is important if your dog's diet doesn't include bones. Adult dogs need about 800 to 1,000 mg of calcium per pound of meat, as calcium should be proportionate to phosphorus. Ideally, between 1:1 and 2:1. Diets high in meat require more calcium, mainly because beef contains a lot of phosphorus.

Creating a calcium supplement from eggshells is a straightforward and empowering process. Start by boiling whole eggshell pieces for 10-15 minutes, then strain and transfer to a baking sheet. Dry the eggshells in an oven at 300°F for at least 10 minutes to eliminate potentially harmful bacteria. Once dry, grind the eggshells into a powder using a blender or food processor. One large eggshell yields about one teaspoon of ground eggshell containing 2,000 mg of calcium. You can confidently serve 1/2 teaspoon of ground shell per pound of beef, knowing you provide the necessary calcium for your dog's diet.

For those seeking alternative sources of calcium, rest assured our homemade bone meal recipe is readily available on page 53. This comprehensive recipe book also references calcium-rich foods, including cottage cheese, sardines, and fresh/canned salmon. Among the leafy greens, spinach is the most calcium-rich, containing 260 mg of calcium per 1 cup cooked. With these readily available options, you can ensure your dog's calcium needs are met without worry.

Chapter 3:

HARMFUL INGREDIENTS AND OTHER CONCERNS

In the early morning, while everything else remains still, a kitchen becomes a hub of activity dedicated to preparing balanced dog meals. The tasks include chopping vegetables, cooking meats, and carefully adding grains to pots. This preparation goes beyond simple feeding; it involves understanding a dog's nutritional requirements and carefully selecting ingredients. The goal is to feed and nourish our dogs, ensuring they receive all the nutrients for a healthy and energetic life.

3.1 Ingredients That Can Harm Your Dog

Every ingredient has a specific role in dog nutrition. However, some substances, even in small amounts, can disrupt the balance, causing chaos in an otherwise well-coordinated system. This section aims to provide a guide through this unclear terrain, highlighting the dangers often overlooked and ensuring a safe journey through the hazards that may lie ahead.

Common Toxins:

- **Chocolate** contains theobromine and caffeine, which can be highly toxic to dogs. Therefore, it is essential to keep this product away from dogs and other pets to avoid any potential health risks.

- **Xylitol** - It is often found in many sugar-free products; xylitol in large amounts is highly toxic to dogs and can cause liver failure.

- **Grapes and Raisins** - It is important to note these fruits can cause dog kidney failure.

- **Onions and Garlic** - Contain thiosulphate, which can cause anemia.

- **Avocados** - Contains Persin, which can cause vomiting and diarrhea.

- **Alcohol** - Even small amounts can cause vomiting, diarrhea, intoxication, and central nervous system issues.

- **Caffeine** - Found in coffee, tea, soda, and energy drinks, can be toxic and potentially fatal.

- **Macadamia Nuts** - Can cause weakness, depression, vomiting, tremors, and hyperthermia. (Avoid most nuts, peanuts, and peanut butter; they are okay to have in moderation. Nuts have a high-fat content, and too much fat can cause complications like pancreatitis.)

- **Dough (Raw Yeast)** - Can expand in the stomach, causing pain and potentially twisting the stomach. The alcohol byproduct from fermentation can also be toxic.

- **Salt and Salty Snack Foods** - Excessive amounts can lead to ion poisoning, which causes symptoms like vomiting, diarrhea, tremors, and seizures.

- **Fatty Foods** - Can cause pancreatitis.

"It is important to review this list and realize that many of these items shouldn't be on our top hits list: alcohol, caffeine, raw dough, salty snack foods, fatty foods. These are things to avoid, so naturally, we should also keep these away from our pets."

Home items like cleaning products, medications, and decorative plants can contain toxic elements and pose health risks.

Plants:

- **Lilies** (For cats especially, but also can be harmful to dogs)
- **Sago Palm** - Extremely toxic, can cause vomiting, diarrhea, seizures, liver failure, and potentially death.
- **Rhododendrons and Azalea** - contain toxins that can cause vomiting, diarrhea, coma, and even death.
- **Tulips and Hyacinths** - The bulbs contain toxins that can cause intense stomach upset, drooling, loss of appetite, convulsions, and cardiac abnormalities.
- **Oleander** - Highly toxic, can cause severe vomiting, slowed heart rate, and possibly death.

Chemicals and Medications:

- **Antifreeze (Ethylene Glycol)** - Even small amounts are highly toxic.
- **Rat Poison** - This can cause severe symptoms, including internal bleeding, kidney failure, and death.
- **NSAIDs (e.g., Ibuprofen, Naproxen)** - Non-steroidal anti-inflammatory drugs can cause gastrointestinal ulcers and kidney failure.
- **Acetaminophen (e.g., Tylenol)** - Can damage red blood cells and cause liver failure.
- **Antidepressants** - These can cause neurological problems like sedation, incoordination, tremors, and seizures.
- **ADD/ADHD Medications** - Can cause tremors, seizures, cardiac problems, and death.
- **De-icing Salts** - Used on roads during winter, can cause skin irritation and, if ingested, lead to severe electrolyte imbalances. Clean off the paws after a walk in the winter! Don't let your pup lick off the salt when back on the warm carpet in front of the fire. It isn't safe in small doses, and doing

it twice a day can be dangerous.

Reading Labels

As dog owners, practice reading the labels of pet foods and treats. Avoid additives like BHA, BHT, and artificial colors that may risk your pet's health. By identifying and avoiding these potentially harmful ingredients, you can make informed choices and prioritize your dog's health over appearance or shelf life. Additionally, regularly reevaluating the foods you feed your dog is crucial to their overall health. Commercial dog foods' formulations are continually changing, making it challenging to stay informed. Therefore, make it a habit to examine the products you select for your pet. Doing so can ensure you provide your dogs with safe and nutritious food, promoting their well-being.

Emergency Response

Despite our best efforts, accidents happen, and dogs, with their curious natures, sometimes ingest substances they should not. In these moments, knowledge transforms into action, guiding the immediate steps to mitigate potential harm. The first and perhaps most crucial action is recognizing the signs of toxin ingestion, which can range from vomiting and diarrhea to more severe symptoms such as seizures or lethargy. Upon suspicion of toxic ingestion, immediately contact a veterinarian or a pet poison hotline. Time often plays a critical role in the effectiveness of treatment, making prompt action paramount. Treatment may involve inducing vomiting under professional guidance or rushing to the nearest veterinary clinic for emergency care. Having on hand a dog first aid kit, complete with activated charcoal—a treatment for certain types of poisoning—can provide an immediate tool in these critical moments.

Yes, there really is such a thing as a dog first aid kit. If you need to get more familiar with it, go to a pet store or online or ask your vet for a recommendation for your dog. It is like insurance…you may never need it, but if you do, you will be happy; it is right there at your fingertips in a moment of high stress.

3.2 Understanding Allergies and Food Sensitivities in Dogs

Canine allergies can be challenging to handle, as they involve a multidisciplinary approach of careful observation, proactive measures, and practical adjustments. Allergies and sensitivities in dogs can cause more than just discomfort; they may indicate an imbalance in the dog's health that requires attention. Recognizing the signs of allergies is vital to initiating a journey that requires patience and persistence. Effective dietary management is important; each decision is critical to a dog's well-being.

Identifying Allergies

Allergies in dogs often cloak themselves in symptoms that could easily be mistaken for lesser ailments. Itchy skin, constant scratching, ear infections, or gastrointestinal disturbances such as vomiting and diarrhea, while seemingly benign, are often harbingers of a more profound discord. More subtle signs might include paw licking, scooting, or even chronic conditions like asthma, pointing towards an immune system in disarray. Understanding these signals of allergies is the first step toward relief.

Common Allergens

Certain ingredients stand out in the landscape of allergens that can disrupt the delicate balance of a dog's health. Proteins, often hailed as the cornerstone of nutrition, are the most common culprits. Beef, dairy, chicken, and even lamb, staples of many canine diets, can become sources of distress. Grains, too, hold a place on this list, with wheat and corn leading the charge. Their presence in many commercial diets makes avoidance a challenge. It is not the ingredient but the immune system's perception that dictates the allergic response, transforming nourishment into a nemesis.

People often use a systematic technique called the elimination and reintroduction method to identify allergens. This method involves gradually removing all ingredients except the most fundamental ones from the diet, generally consisting of a single protein and carbohydrate source. As the symptoms decrease over several weeks, people gradually reintroduce fresh ingredients, one at a time, while closely monitoring the body's reaction to each addition. This practice is a measured and purposeful approach that helps pinpoint the allergen. It provides a way to create a diet that avoids these triggers, ultimately resulting in a life free from allergic discomfort.

Tailoring Diets

Crafting a diet plan for a dog with allergies or sensitivities requires customization and creativity. Avoiding the allergens is not enough, as you must also provide the necessary nutritional requirements while avoiding known triggers. To achieve this, novel proteins and alternative carbohydrates become the foundation of this new diet, as they offer essential nutrients without the risk of allergic reactions. Some examples of novel proteins include venison, rabbit, or kangaroo, paired with carbohydrates like sweet potatoes or peas. In addition, supplements may be necessary to compensate for any potential gaps in nutrition, such as those for digestive support, skin health, or overall vitality. This tailored approach alleviates symptoms and provides a roadmap to a life of comfort and enjoyment, free from the shadows of allergic reactions.

Remember, allergies are not always to foods. When in doubt or if the systemic test doesn't locate the issue, consider the season. For airborne allergens, consider anything you have introduced to the house, such as new carpeting. Consider new dog toys or even the detergent you use to wash their blankets and towels.

Professional Help

Professional help is vital when managing allergies and sensitivities in dogs. Experienced veterinarians can test your dog's allergies using blood or skin prick tests to identify specific allergens. With this information, they can help you create a diet that avoids these allergens while still meeting your dog's nutritional needs.

Veterinarians are more than just advisors - they become partners in helping your dog feel better. By working together, you can help restore your dog's joy of eating and replace discomfort with delight.

3.3 Organic vs. Non-Organic

The choice between organic and non-organic ingredients in dog nutrition is complex and requires careful consideration of various factors. In addition to their immediate health benefits, organic foods offer a sanctuary of purity in an age of chemical ubiquity. They are cultivated without synthetic pesticides, herbicides, or genetically modified organisms (GMOs), lowering the risk of toxin exposure for dogs and ecosystems. Organic farming practices also champion soil health and biodiversity, contributing to a legacy of environmental conservation. However, the cost of organic foods is frequently higher due to the stringent standards of organic farming. While this can be a deterrent for some pet owners, the investment in quality can pay off in the long run. High-quality, organic ingredients offer enhanced nutritional content, no harmful chemicals, and the potential for long-term health benefits. Dogs who consume such diets may experience fewer health issues related to toxin exposure or nutritional deficiencies, ultimately reducing veterinary expenses and extending their quality of life. Make sure to consider the value of health over time when making the cost versus quality calculus.

Understanding Organic Labeling

Feeding our dogs the best food possible is always our top priority. However, buying organic dog food can be challenging and expensive. But there is good news. We can find a balance by purchasing organic foods commonly grown with pesticides, such as apples and spinach. We can opt for non-organic versions of other foods that don't have as many pesticides. Another way to save money is to buy organic food gradually and keep an eye on sales or seasonal deals. This way, we can keep our dogs healthy and safe from harmful substances while supporting farmers who grow food in an environmentally friendly way.

Organic certification labels indicate compliance with specific standards set by certifying bodies. These labels include '100% Organic,' 'Organic,' and 'Made with Organic Ingredients.' The highest standard is '100% Organic,' meaning all ingredients are certified organic. 'Organic' permits the addition of a small percentage of non-organic ingredients to a list of approved substances. 'Made with Organic Ingredients' requires at least 70% certified organic ingredients.

However, it is important to note the reliability of a product's organic commitment depends on its manufacturer's honesty and transparency.

Chapter 4:

CREATING A ROTATIONAL MENU FOR NUTRITIONAL VARIETY

Think of your dog's meal plan as a fun story where every ingredient adds something special. This way of feeding, rotational feeding, mixes things up to ensure your dog gets all the nutrients it needs. It's not just about trying new things for fun. Different foods bring different health benefits, and changing your dog's diet can help prevent allergies. Eating the same thing all the time might lead to food sensitivities. Still, your dog is less likely to develop these issues with a mix of different proteins and carbs. So, this method is like a superhero for your dog's health, fighting against boredom and keeping allergies at bay.

How to Make a Rotational Menu for Your Dog

Creating a rotating menu for your dog might sound complex. Still, it's all about knowing what's good and adding variety. We will start with a few essential meals focusing on a different protein, like chicken or beef, and add a mix of veggies and grains. Then, plan out when to serve each meal, changing it daily and weekly. This schedule is flexible; you can adjust it based on what's available or what your dog likes best.

How to Introduce New Foods

Adding new foods to your dog's diet should be done gently, like planting a new seed in a garden. Mix some of the latest food with what your dog usually eats. Watch how your dog reacts to the change. If everything looks good, you can gradually add more. If not, it's back to the drawing board, but that's okay. It's all about finding what works best for your dog without causing any upset. I can remember when I first started this meal plan. I was so nervous about adding this food or that food. Would she like it…spit it out, walk away from her bowl, and give me that 'what did you do' look. Would some foods or combinations make her sick or at least give her an upset tummy? What the heck am I doing? But I persevered, we worked together, and now she eats her favorites and some not-so-favorites, and we have a program and plan down pat.

Keeping an Eye on Your Dog's Health and Preferences

As you try out this rotational diet, pay close attention to how your dog responds. Look for signs of good health, like a shiny coat and plenty of energy, and notice which meals they get excited about. Your observations will help you tweak the menu over time. This way, the diet keeps evolving based on what makes your dog happiest and healthiest.

In essence, creating a rotational menu for your dog is about more than just feeding them different things. It's a commitment to their health, happiness, and overall well-being, ensuring every meal contributes to a life full of zest and vitality.

4.1 7-Day Meal Plan

We want to ensure our dogs are healthy and happy. One crucial way to do this is by feeding them a well-balanced diet that gives them all the necessary nutrients. However, planning and preparing meals for our dogs can be challenging, especially when we're busy. Luckily, there are some easy ways to make meal planning easier. We can create a flexible meal plan that includes a variety of ingredients to keep things interesting, and we can even use leftovers from our human 'table' meals, ensuring the food is safe and healthy for our dogs. We can also save time by using appliances like slow cookers and preparing ingredients in advance. If we don't have the time or desire to make homemade meals all the time, we can find high-quality commercial foods made with natural ingredients or take a bagged meal from the freezer we have made before and put it away for the future.' The point is to use them so you don't have to make new, fresh meals daily.

It's essential to read the labels and look for products that include meat, vegetables, and whole grains. By providing our dogs with nutritious and tasty meals, we show them how much we love and care for them. Here's a simple template for creating a homemade meal plan focusing on balance and variety. Consult with a veterinarian or a canine nutritionist to ensure the meals fit your dog's health needs and dietary requirements.

Basic Weekly Meal Plan:

Day 1: Beginners Meal: Chicken & Rice Delight
- **Protein:** Cooked chicken breast (no skin or bones)
- **Vegetables:** Spinach, carrots and zucchini
- **Carbs:** Sweet potato (grain-free) or brown rice
- **Supplement:** Consider a teaspoon of flaxseed oil for omega-3 fatty acids

Day 2: Beef & Pumpkin
- **Protein:** Lean ground beef or turkey, cooked
- **Vegetables:** Pureed pumpkin (not pie filling), peas, and carrots
- **Carbs:** Brown rice, oats or quinoa
- **Supplement:** Consider adding bone meal for calcium

Day 3: Turkey and Quinoa Mash

- **Protein:** Ground turkey, cooked
- **Vegetables:** Steamed broccoli
- **Carbs:** Quinoa
- **Supplement:** A fish oil capsule for omega-3

Day 4: Lamb and Greens

- **Protein:** Cooked ground lamb
- **Vegetables:** Spinach or kale (lightly steamed)
- **Carbs:** Couscous
- **Supplement:** Pinch of Cinnamon for Anti-inflammatory properties

Day 5: Fish Dish/Day

- **Protein:** Cooked salmon or tilapia
- **Vegetables:** Green Beans or Chopped zucchini
- **Carbs:** Sweet Potato or Cooked barley
- **Supplement:** Plain, low-fat yogurt, blueberries or fermented vegetables for antioxidants and probiotics

Day 6: Scrambled Eggs and Spinach

- **Protein:** Scrambled eggs
- **Vegetables:** Sauteed spinach and carrots
- **Supplement:** Cottage cheese for calcium or add blueberries for antioxidants

Day 7: Doggie Stew

- **Protein:** A mix of leftover meats from the week
- **Vegetables:** Any leftover veggies, chopped
- **Carbs:** A blend of remaining grains
- **Supplement:** A splash of apple cider vinegar for digestion. Consider

additional supplements at the end of the week, such as multivitamins, probiotics, etc.

General Tips:

- **Variety is vital:** Rotate proteins and veggies to offer a range of nutrients.

- **Balance over time:** Aim for nutritional balance over a week, not each meal.

- **Portion sizes:** Adjust portions based on your dog's size, age, and activity level.

- **Consult professionals:** Check with a vet or nutritionist to customize the plan to your dog's specific needs, especially if your dog has health issues.

- The chef recommends keeping and refrigerating food scraps separately in a resealable container throughout the week to avoid cross-contamination; if the scraps are still good, you will have all the base ingredients for the 'Doggie Stew.'

Remember, this template is a starting point. You can adjust the ingredients and supplements according to your dog's tastes, tolerances, and nutritional requirements.

7-DAY MEAL PLANNER

DAY 1
Meal Plan: _____
Activity Plan: _____

DAY 2
Meal Plan: _____
Activity Plan: _____

DAY 3
Meal Plan: _____
Activity Plan: _____

DAY 4
Meal Plan: _____
Activity Plan: _____

DAY 5
Meal Plan: _____
Activity Plan: _____

DAY 6
Meal Plan: _____
Activity Plan: _____

DAY 7
Meal Plan: _____
Activity Plan: _____

SHOPPING LIST

NOTES

Chapter 5:

EQUIPPING THE BISCUIT CHEF

In the soft glow of the morning kitchen, where the scent of coffee mingles with the quiet start of the day, the kitchen becomes more than just a room. It's where the simple act of preparing meals for our canine friends turns into an expression of love and care. Every ingredient, tool, and recipe purposefully transforms essential components into nourishing meals. This space is where pet owners dedicate themselves to the health and happiness of their dogs, using nutrition as their guide and their affection as the secret ingredient.

The Home Chef's Toolkit: Essentials for Preparing Dog Food

Necessities Over Niceties

Cooking healthy meals for your pets doesn't have to be complicated or require fancy kitchen equipment. You only need good-quality knives, pots, pans, cutting boards, mixing bowls, measuring cups and spoons, and resealable storage containers. Lots and lots of resealable storage containers. A sharp knife can easily cut through vegetables and meats, keeping all the good stuff inside. The cutting board is where you do all the chopping and preparing, and mixing bowls help you blend everything, and large pots for batch cooking. All are essential for anyone who wants to make tasty and nutritious meals for their dogs.

(*Chef Tip on Knife selection:* An 8-inch chef knife should work for most individuals. If you have larger hands or are taller than average, opt for a larger size for better knife handling, something most people don't consider, but if you have ever been an eight-hour-a-day chef, this is more important than the many other tools in your arsenal.)

Specialized Equipment

When cooking food for dogs, it's always good to have modern equipment to make things easier. For example, a food processor or blender can help us make healthy purees from fruits and veggies full of vitamins and minerals for our dogs. A large pot or slow cooker is another excellent tool that can help us simmer meats and retain all the flavors and nutrients, making them easy for our pups to digest. Air fryers are a great way to make quick and easy dehydrated snacks. These items are best because they make cooking for our dogs simpler and more effective while still keeping the traditional way of preparing food. Always keep an eye out for other more efficient ways to use standard equipment to simplify the cooking process. If you use it for your human family, odds are you can use it for your furry accomplices.

Investment in Quality

Investing in high-quality kitchen tools may initially seem expensive, but it's a wise investment in the long run. This, of course, is the same advice you always hear for your kitchen adventures. These tools are built to last and can save money by avoiding frequent replacements and repairs. For example, a cheap blender might need help with daily use and break down quickly. In contrast, a high-quality blender can withstand the demands of processing harsh ingredients. Though it may cost more upfront, investing in quality tools can save you the frustration and inefficiency of using inadequate ones. If you have taken this advice, you likely already have the equipment and quality equipment you need for the pooch experiment.

Cleanliness and Maintenance

The kitchen is the heart of meal preparation, where cleanliness is crucial for maintaining a safe cooking environment. Proper cleaning of kitchen tools is vital to prevent cross-contamination and ensure the safety of humans and pets. You can use 1/2 fl. oz or 15 ml of bleach per one gallon of room-temperature water to clean cutting boards and equipment. Items like cutting boards can be soaked in this solution if filthy or used hard in the last go-round. All surfaces should be wiped down thoroughly with solution, especially after handling uncooked meat, unwashed fruits, and vegetables. Regular upkeep of kitchen tools extends their lifespan and protects the cook's and their pets' health. Remember to keep knives sharp and rust-free and replace rusty equipment or utensils.

Equipment Checklist

- 8-10 Inch Chef Knife
- Honing Steel
- Sharpening Tool/Stone
- Utility Knife (less than 6 in)
- Paring Knife
- 1 Set Measuring Cups
- 1 Set Measuring Spoons
- 1 Set Spatulas
- Cutting Boards
- Mixing Bowls
- Large Pot for batch cooking and boiling
- Storage Containers

- Sauté Pans
- Food Processor or Blender (Optional)
- Slow Cooker (Optional)
- Dehydrator Air Fryer (Optional)

Storing Safely

Ensuring food safety and extending its shelf life requires a little practice with homemade dog food. Always follow food-safe practices. The following are some instructions on safely storing your homemade dog food, focusing on refrigeration and freezing, choosing the proper containers, and recognizing when food has spoiled. If the food doesn't look or smell good, toss it. The small amount of tossed food is nothing compared to the potential for making your pup ill. And if you can't see or smell anything unusual, use better judgment. If you wouldn't use a leftover over a week old for yourself, don't use it for your pup. Remember, this all starts as human food, so use human food rules and judgment for keeping or tossing. It only becomes dog food when it hits their bowl.

Refrigeration

Temperature Maintenance: Keep your refrigerator at or below 40°F (4°C). This temperature slows bacterial growth and helps keep the food safe.

- **Storage Duration:** Store homemade dog food in the fridge for three days to avoid bacterial growth.
- **Containers for Fridge:** Use airtight containers to minimize exposure to air. Glass or BPA-free plastic containers are recommended.

Freezing
- **Rapid Cooling:** It's important to cool food down before freezing. Placing the food in the refrigerator after cooking will help reduce the formation of ice crystals that can harm its quality and prevent food-borne illness.
- **Portioning:** Divide the food into meal-sized portions. Portioning makes thawing easier and prevents the need to refreeze leftovers. It also allows

you to do an inventory count to know how many servings you have of each combination/meal, thus letting you know when to prep another batch.

- **Container Selection:** Opt for airtight, freezer-safe containers, such as glass containers, which are ideal because they are non-reactive. However, BPA-free plastic is a lighter alternative. Not all 'baggies' and food storage bags are BFA-free. Read the packaging; if you don't see it, assume it isn't there. Ensure lids fit securely.

- **Freezing Duration:** You can freeze and store homemade dog food for up to six months. However, use it within the first three months for the best quality.

- **Labeling:** Always label your containers with the freeze date to keep track of storage durations, as well as the 'best use by date---90 days' and the 'last use by date--- 180 days'. That way, everything is clear when you go into the freezer at any given time.

Recognizing Spoilage

- **Smell:** An off or sour smell is a primary indicator of spoilage.
- **Visual Signs:** Look out for discoloration or mold growth on the food.
- **Texture Changes:** Any sliminess or hardness not characteristic of the food's original texture suggests spoilage.
- **Taste:** Sometimes, food on the verge of spoilage hasn't given off any odor or visual cues. Taste a tiny bit of food. If it's soured, throw it away.
- **Action:** If you detect any spoilage, discard the food immediately to prevent health risks to your dog.

Labeling and Organizing

Creating homemade dog food is a labor of love. Label containers, prioritize rotation, and use stackable containers. Make the food easily accessible and track consumption. These practices create a personalized dietary history and ensure optimal health outcomes, fortifying the health of our beloved companions. Follow these tips to ensure your dog's food is safe and healthy.

Always use clean hands and utensils when handling ingredients and preparing food. Thaw frozen dog food in the refrigerator instead of at room temperature to minimize bacterial growth. Serve the food at room temperature once it's thawed, and discard any uneaten food after 30 minutes. Yes, it is a fair amount of work, but nothing more than you would typically do for your own foods in the fridge or freezer or before preparing them for dinner. Please keep that in mind when you are concerned about all the 'extra work" involved in doing a good thing for your pets.

Chapter 6:

TRANSITIONING: INTRODUCING HOMEMADE MEALS

As we introduce our dogs to homemade meals, we're not just changing their diet but deepening our care for them. This transition, meal preparation with our hands, signifies a profound shift in nurturing our canine friends. It expresses love and a commitment to improving their well-being through nutrition.

6.1 Special Dog Breed Considerations

When it comes to feeding dogs, one size does not fit all. Different breeds have unique dietary considerations based on size, energy levels, and specific health predispositions resulting from their physical design. Here is a detailed list of the top 25 dog breeds and their diet considerations:

Labrador Retriever
- **Prone to obesity:** Monitor calorie intake closely.

- **High energy:** Requires a diet rich in proteins and fats for energy.

German Shepherd

- **Sensitive digestion:** May benefit from easily digestible foods.
- **Joint issues:** Look for diets supplemented with glucosamine and chondroitin.

Golden Retriever

- **Risk of cancer:** An Antioxidant-rich diet may help prevent cancer.
- **Tendency towards obesity and hip dysplasia:** Ensure a balanced diet and healthy weight.

French Bulldog

- **Risk of obesity:** Monitor portion sizes and avoid overfeeding.
- **Breathing issues:** Avoid foods that can cause gas or bloating.

Bulldog

- **Skin allergies:** May require a diet with limited ingredients or hypoallergenic food.
- **Chewing difficulties:** Prefer soft, wet foods or small kibble sizes.

Poodle

- **Prone to dental issues:** Regular dental chews and dry food can help maintain oral health.
- **Active lifestyle:** Needs a protein-rich diet to support energy levels.

Beagle

- **Prone to obesity:** Carefully measure food and limit treats.
- **Energetic:** Requires a balanced diet to support an active lifestyle.

Rottweiler

- **Joint health:** Diets with joint-supporting nutrients like omega-3 fatty acids are beneficial.

- **Muscle maintenance:** Follow a high-protein diet to promote and maintain muscle strength.

Yorkshire Terrier

- **Dental issues:** Small breeds are often prone to dental problems, so that crunchy foods can help.
- **Sensitive stomach:** May benefit from a diet with easy-to-digest ingredients.

Boxer

- **Heart health:** Look for foods rich in taurine and L-carnitine.
- **High energy:** Needs a diet with plenty of protein and carbohydrates for energy.

Siberian Husky

- **High energy:** Requires a diet of fats and proteins.
- **Sensitive stomachs:** Some do better on grain-free diets.

Dachshund

- **Prone to obesity and back issues:** Keep them lean to reduce stress on their spine.
- **Joint health:** Supplements like glucosamine can be beneficial.

Great Dane

- **Bloat risk:** Feed smaller frequent meals to prevent bloat.
- **Bone health:** Needs diets with appropriate calcium-to-phosphorus ratio to support bone growth. (See beginner's guide on raw food for more information.)

Doberman Pinscher

- **Cardiovascular health:** Requires taurine and omega-3 fatty acids to support heart health.
- **High energy:** Needs a nutrient-rich diet to fuel their active lifestyle.

Australian Shepherd

- **High energy:** The diet should support their active lifestyle with enough protein and fat.
- **Joint health:** Consider foods with added glucosamine for joint support.

Miniature Schnauzer

- **Prone to pancreatitis:** Low-fat diets are often recommended.
- **Urinary stones:** They may require a diet that helps manage mineral levels.

Pembroke Welsh Corgi

- **Weight management:** Prone to obesity, so monitor calorie intake.
- **Joint health:** Supplements like omega-3 fatty acids can support joint health.

Cavalier King Charles Spaniel

- **Heart health:** Benefit from diets with taurine and omega-3 fatty acids.
- **Weight management:** Monitor their diet to prevent obesity, which can stress their heart.

Shih Tzu

- **Allergies:** You may need a hypoallergenic diet to avoid skin and digestive issues.
- **Dental health:** Small breeds benefit from chews and crunchy foods.

Boston Terrier

- **Gas issues:** This may require an easy diet on the stomach to prevent flatulence.
- **Eye health:** Antioxidants like lutein and vitamin A can support eye health.

Chihuahua

- **Prone to Obesity:** Small breeds like Chihuahuas have less room for extra calories, so monitoring their food intake and keeping treats to a minimum is crucial.

- **Dental Health:** Chihuahuas are prone to dental issues. Dry kibble and crunchy treats can help reduce tartar build-up.
- **Hypoglycemia Risk:** Due to their small size, they can be prone to low blood sugar. Small, frequent meals can help maintain blood sugar levels.

Border Collie

- **High Energy:** Active working dogs require diets rich in protein and fats to fuel their energy needs.
- **Joint Health:** With their high activity levels, incorporating foods with joint-supporting nutrients like glucosamine can be beneficial.
- **Mental Stimulation:** Omega-3 fatty acids found in fish oils can support brain health, complementing their mental engagement needs.

Cocker Spaniel

- **Ear Health:** Dogs are prone to ear infections, and maintaining a proper diet can help prevent issues. Avoid excessive moisture, and check dogs' ears regularly.
- **Weight Management:** If overfed, dogs can quickly gain weight. A balanced diet and regular exercise are essential.

Akita

- **Large Breed Nutrition:** A diet for large breeds is required to support joint health and maintain healthy growth rates.
- **Bloat Risk:** Like other large breeds, Akitas can be susceptible to bloat. Feed smaller and more frequent meals.
- **Coat Health:** Rich in oils, their thick coat benefits from diets high in omega-3 and omega-6 fatty acids for shine and health.

Bichon Frise

- **Allergies and Sensitivities:** People often have sensitive skin and stomachs. A hypoallergenic or limited-ingredient diet may prevent allergic reactions.

- **Bladder Stones:** Prone to urinary issues, including bladder stones. Maintaining hydration and considering diets low in purines can help.

Scottish Terrier

- Von Willebrand's Disease affects blood clotting. While diet cannot prevent it, awareness of the condition is vital for overall health management.

- **Skin Conditions:** For people prone to skin allergies, a diet rich in fatty acids can support skin health and reduce irritation.

- **Cancer Risks:** Scottish Terriers are at higher risk of certain cancers. Diets rich in antioxidants help support overall health and longevity.

If you have a breed not listed above, see your vet or a nutrition specialist or go online to a board that discusses your breed for more detailed information. There are hundreds of breeds and mixed breeds; thus, getting the proper information for your pup is important for the long haul.

6.2 How to Gradually Introduce Homemade Food

Phased Introduction

When introducing homemade food to your dog's diet, do it gradually. Start by adding a small portion mixed with regular kibble. Increase the homemade portion with each meal until it replaces the old diet. Allow your dog time to adjust to the new diet. When combining the two diets, consider the textures to spark your dog's curiosity and encourage engagement.

Observation Is Key

When changing your dog's diet, paying close attention to their behavior and reaction to the food is essential. You can observe your dog's response to the food by noticing if they wag their tail or lean towards their bowl while eating, indicating they like the food. On the other hand, if they show hesitation or indifference, you might need to adjust the food's flavor, texture, or ingredients to make it more appealing to them or move on to the next ingredient/combination of foods. Some foods will just be an issue for some pups.

Observing your dog's behavior ensures your homemade meals meet their preferences and needs. For example, suppose you notice an increase in your dog's energy levels after introducing homemade food to their diet. In that case, it is a sign the new food positively impacts their health and well-being.

Adjustment Period

Every dog is unique and has its own preferences and digestive system. So, when changing your dog's diet, patience is vital. Some dogs might take to the new diet immediately, while others might be more cautious and unsure. It's essential to give your dog time to adjust to the new diet at its own pace so that it can adapt without stress or pressure.

To make the transition easier, you can introduce a new flavor to your dog's food by mixing a small amount of homemade bone broth. The broth will help your dog get used to the new taste in a familiar context and make it less intimidating. It's like how humans might try a small bite of a new dish before fully committing to it. This way, your dog can be curious and cautious without feeling overwhelmed by the change.

Consistency Matters

Consistency is essential when adjusting your dog to a new diet. Stick to a daily feeding routine and gradually introduce new ingredients to their meals. Doing this creates a sense of stability for your dog, which can help them feel secure during the transition. Just like our daily routines provide comfort and strength, consistency in your dog's feeding schedule can help them feel more at ease amidst changes.

DIET TRANSITION DIARY

*This printable page is designed to track
the gradual introduction of homemade food into your dog's diet.*

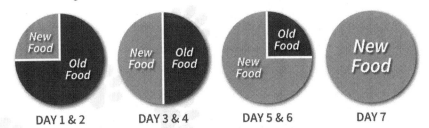

| DAY 1 & 2 | DAY 3 & 4 | DAY 5 & 6 | DAY 7 |

__/__	Reactions	Preferences	Behavior & Physical Condition
DAY 1			
DAY 2			
DAY 3			
DAY 4			
DAY 5			
DAY 6			
DAY 7			

A friend of a professional acquaintance of mine reviewed my book and shared his experience of preparing homemade food for his dogs. In addition to having three active teenagers, they owned three very active dogs: a 90-pound boxer, a 50-pound lab, and a 25-pound dachshund. They used to feed them commercial-bagged kibble for many years, but after discussing it with other dog owners, they switched to homemade dog food. As a result, all three of their dogs lived well beyond 14 years old, which is impressive, especially for boxers. They still prepare homemade dog food for their current dog.

6.3 Monitoring Your Dog's Health During the Transition

There are many different approaches to feeding dogs. Some people make their dog food, while others buy commercial options. However, the best approach may lie somewhere in the middle. We can provide our dogs with a balanced and diverse diet that meets all their nutritional needs by carefully selecting ingredients and nutrients to keep them healthy, happy, and well-fed. It's like a dance, where we aim to create the perfect meal for our furry companions so they can enjoy their food and stay healthy for years.

Stool Surveillance

When we give our dogs new food, we must pay attention to their stool. Their stool's consistency, color, and frequency can tell us much about their digestive health and whether their new diet works for them. For example, the new diet might suit their digestion if their stool becomes firmer. But if their stool suddenly becomes runny or changes color, it could mean they're not tolerating the new food well, and we should rethink their diet. It may seem small, but paying attention to these changes is vital to caring for our dogs and ensuring they're healthy. When introducing new ingredients to their diet, we must watch their droppings to see how they react to each new thing.

Weight and Appetite Tracking

When we change our dog's food, it affects their weight and appetite. Keeping track of these changes can tell us if the new food makes our dog healthy and happy. If our dog's weight changes gradually and healthily, the food benefits them. And if our dogs are eager to eat their meals, they like the food and are doing well. On the other hand, if our dog loses interest in their food, it could mean they don't like it, or it's not good for them. Keeping a record of these changes helps us understand what foods are best for our dogs.

Behavioral Changes

When we change our dog's diet, we can watch for more than just changes in their poop. We can also look for changes in their behavior, such as if they become more playful or stressed out. These changes can give us clues about whether the new diet is good for them or not if they seem happier, more energetic, and more playful. But if they seem tired, less playful, or stressed, we might need to rethink their diet. It can take time and attention to notice these changes. Still, it's worth it because it helps us understand how our dog's diet affects their emotional and mental well-being.

As a biscuit chef, keeping track of observations and ideas is part of improving our craft. I recommend utilizing the notes section on the meal plan page. It's the perfect place to jot down your thoughts and track what's working and what's not. Remember to take advantage of this helpful tool!

6.4 Dealing with Picky Eaters: Tips and Tricks

If you have a picky-eating dog, it can be challenging to know what to feed it. But with some patience, creativity, and consistency, you can create a mealtime routine your dog will love, providing it with the nutrition it needs. It's like a dance, where you mix different flavors and textures to create the perfect balance.

Establishing a consistent routine during mealtime can help picky eaters feel more secure and open to trying new foods. This routine should be relaxed and comforting, creating a designated space where your pet feels safe and undisturbed. This consistency helps them engage with their food, savor each new flavor and texture, and appreciate their mealtime experience. Sticking to this routine can help your pet feel more comfortable changing their diet and make the transition easier. It's essential to do so slowly and gradually when introducing new foods. Positive reinforcement is also crucial to making mealtime a fun experience for your dog. By rewarding them with praise and treats, you can create positive associations between mealtimes and pleasure, encouraging your dog to be more curious and adventurous with his/her food.

6.5 Balancing Homemade and Commercial Foods: Finding the Middle Ground

Regarding feeding dogs, there are two main types of diets: homemade and commercial. But did you know there's a perfect middle ground that combines the best of both worlds? By carefully balancing the ingredients in our dogs' meals, we can ensure they get all the nutrients they need for a healthy and happy life. It's like a special recipe that gives our pups a variety of tasty foods that also help keep them strong and full of energy. It's a bit of a science, but seeing our dogs thrive is worth it!

Nutritional Complement

When selecting commercial foods to complement homemade meals, it's essential to look beyond marketing claims and choose ingredients that fill gaps in the nutrient profile. Understanding the nutrients from homemade meals allows you to select commercial foods that provide specific vitamins or minerals, creating a complete and harmonious dietary ensemble that supports your dog's overall health and well-being.

Transition Strategies

Navigating the transition to a diet that includes homemade and commercial foods necessitates flexible and responsive strategies for the dog's needs. For dogs with specific health conditions or dietary preferences, this transition might involve gradually introducing homemade meals, closely monitored to gauge tolerance and acceptance. It's a process that respects the dog's pace, allowing for adjustments and modifications that cater to their needs.

In instances where health conditions dictate a nuanced approach to diet, homemade meals might be tailored to address these needs directly, with commercial foods serving as a nutritional safety net, assuring a complete diet. This tailored approach, profoundly personal and considerate of the dog's health and preferences, ensures the transition to a combined diet is successful and sustainable in the long term.

Consultation with Nutritionists

There are several ways to feed our beloved pets. Some prefer preparing their dog's food, while others choose commercial options mixed with kibble. However, the best approach may be in the middle, where you can offer your dogs a balanced and diverse diet that meets all their nutritional requirements by carefully selecting ingredients and nutrients to keep our dogs healthy, happy, and well-fed.

6.6 When to Consult a Vet: Signs to Watch For

When feeding our fur babies, we want to do everything possible to keep them healthy. We pay close attention to what they eat and how they react, especially when we switch up their food. It's well known that even small changes in their diet can significantly impact their overall health. That's why it's good to know when to ask a vet for help if you are unsure what to do. They can help us navigate challenges to ensure our dogs are well-fed and happy. No 'sign' is too small to ask questions or ask for help in assessing a situation.

Unexpected Reactions

Switching to a new diet for your dog can sometimes cause unexpected problems. Your dog might show discomfort, such as scratching, rashes, or digestive issues like vomiting or unusual tiredness. These signs signal something is wrong, and you should take your dog to a veterinarian for help. Veterinarians can figure out what's causing these signs and help your dog feel better. It could be that your dog's body doesn't like a particular ingredient in the new diet, or there might be an underlying health issue that the latest diet has uncovered. Often, it is an allergy to a specific food or ingredient, so no problem is too small to be discussed and resolved with the vet.

Nutritional Deficiencies

It's essential to pay attention to the nutrients we get from our food, even if we're trying to eat healthier. Sometimes, we might not get everything we need, which can cause problems with our bodies. If our pets have a dull coat, dental issues, low energy levels, or get sick, it could mean they're missing the correct nutrients in their diet.

Customization of Diet

Sometimes, our dogs might have special dietary needs or health conditions that require a special diet. A veterinarian can create a customized diet to suit our dog's taste buds and address their health needs.

This process involves a lot of observation, testing, and collaboration between pet owners and vets. By working together, we can adjust the diet to help our dogs stay healthy and recover from health issues. It's not just about feeding our dogs anymore—it's about ensuring they're healthy, happy, and well-taken care of before they get sick.

Regular Check-Ins

We should regularly visit the vet to keep track of our dog's weight, appetite, behavior, and overall health. During these visits, we can discuss concerns and get advice on adjusting our dog's diet. This partnership between pet owners and veterinarians ensures our dogs get the best possible care.

Changing our dog's diet can be a complex process. Still, we can ensure our furry friends receive the best nutrition and care by working together and being attentive, compassionate, and collaborative.

Chapter 7:

BATCH COOKING RECIPE SAVING TIME AND ENERGY

Batch cooking simplifies homemade dog food preparation, making it efficient and meaningful. This approach combines planning, bulk preparation, strategic freezing, and versatile mix-and-match meal creation to ensure dogs enjoy nutritious, varied meals without daily cooking. Here are some steps and beliefs to consider when utilizing this technique.

- **Planning:** Important for efficiency, planning outlines the meals' components—proteins, vegetables, grains—according to your dog's nutritional needs, setting the stage for a smooth cooking process.

- **Bulk Cooking:** This step involves cooking large quantities of food simultaneously. The process becomes more manageable and time-efficient by organizing tasks (e.g., chopping vegetables, then portioning meats) and grouping ingredients by cooking time.

- **Freezing Portions:** After cooking, meals are quickly cooled and divided into portions that match your dog's feeding routine. Proper freezing techniques and suitable containers are crucial for preserving the food's quality, ensuring meals remain fresh and nutritious until served. One additional point here. If you are serving based on serving weight, using freezer bags or other containers that hold roughly the amount of a single serving is important. Why? You don't want leftovers to have to refreeze (if you even can) and create potential health issues. Make your life simple. One serving to a container.

- **Mix and Match:** This strategy adds variety and nutritional balance by allowing different combinations of meal components. It adapts to changes in your dog's taste or dietary needs, showcasing the flexibility and benefits of batch cooking.

How to Prepare Sweet Potatoes Effectively

Boiling is the best method for effectively preparing sweet potatoes. Simply boil whole sweet potatoes until they are soft, then allow them to cool. The peel will easily come off after cooking, so discard the trimmed ends and dice the skins to incorporate them back into the mashed sweet potatoes. Combine ingredients in a large mixing bowl.

Additionally baking whole sweet potatoes for 45-60 minutes at 400°F (204°C). takes longer but enhances overal flavor and provides a firmer texture.

Nutritional Batch Cooking Recipe for Dogs

It's important to remember the recipe provided is only a general guideline. Adjust the portions according to your dog's weight, activity level, and any specific health concerns. To ensure this meal plan suits your dog's dietary requirements, it's always best to consult a veterinarian or a pet nutritionist. The recipe provides a balanced diet with a good mix of protein, carbohydrates, and vegetables. For protein, chicken is the primary source, brown rice is for carbs, and a blend of vegetables for fiber and vitamins.

Equipment: Cooking utensils such as big pots, a cutting board with a knife, measuring cups, and containers for freezing.

Downloadable Recipies

NUTRITIONAL BATCH RECIPE

- CAL / SERVING: ~286
- PROTEIN: 31 g
- CARBOHYDRATES: 23 g
- FAT: 5.5 g
- FIBER: 2.7 g
- SERVINGS: 16

INGREDIENTS

- ☐ 5 pounds of boneless, skinless chicken or another high-quality protein
- ☐ 2 cups of uncooked brown rice *(for carbs and fiber)*
- ☐ 1 pound of chopped carrots *(provides fiber and vitamin A)*
- ☐ 1 pound of chopped green beans *(for fiber and vitamins)*
- ☐ 1 sweet potato, peeled and cubed *(for beta-carotene and vitamins)*
- ☐ *Optional: Vet-recommended supplements like calcium or fish oil*

DIRECTIONS

1) Prepare the Protein:

Cook 5 pounds of chicken (or other protein) and then dice, yielding about 12 cups of diced protein.

2) Cook the Rice:

Cook 2 cups of brown rice according to package instructions, yielding about 6 cups of cooked rice.

3) Prepare the Vegetables:

Steam or boil the carrots, green beans, and sweet potatoes, yielding about 6 cups of cooked vegetables.

4) Mix All Ingredients:

Combine all ingredients in a large mixing bowl. This mixture totals about 24 cups of dog food.

5) Portioning and Freezing

For a 50-pound dog, feeding about 2.5 percent of their body weight, you would provide about 1.25 pounds / 1.5 cups of food daily. Divide the mixture into 14 portions of 1.5 cups and freeze in individual containers.

For Smaller Dogs (~25 pounds): Halve the daily portion to about 0.75 cups per day, yielding about 28 servings from this recipe.

For Larger Dogs (~75 pounds): Increase the daily portion to about 2.25 cups per day, yielding roughly 10 servings from this recipe.

7.1 The Power of Bone Broth (recipe)

Bone broth, an ancient remedy, has gained popularity among pet owners as a natural and healthy way to nourish their dogs. Made by simmering bones and marrow, this nutrient-rich elixir offers numerous health benefits for canines. Bone broth is delicious and a soothing balm for the digestive system, making it a versatile ingredient in a dog's diet. Rich in protein, collagen for joint health, and glutamine for gut health, bone broth is a powerhouse of nutrients essential for a dog's well-being. It is one of the reasons we like to give our pups a bone for a snack, even though most people believe it is for brushing and whitening teeth.

Incorporating bone broth into your dog's meals is an excellent way to enhance flavor and nutritional content. Bone broth is a natural and nutritious way to support your dog's health. By including it in your dog's diet in moderation, you can contribute to their long-term well-being, helping them stay healthy, happy, and active for years to come.

Storage Tips

Once the broth cools down, it can be portioned into silicone molds or ice cube trays, making it simple to store and use whenever required. You can keep the frozen cubes in an airtight container in the freezer for up to six months or store them in glass jars in the refrigerator for up to a week. It is a good idea to do both. Use some for immediate use and some for downline. Adding bone broth to your dog's meals makes them more delicious and enjoyable while providing essential nutrients. My wiggle-butt Dot is not a big drinker, but she loves bone broth water. It's a great way to get her to drink in the summer, especially when she has a dry nose! And that brings up another point... dry nose often means insufficient liquids... so this is one way to solve that problem.

Bone Meal Prep

Hold onto those leftover bones from your dog's treats and meals, especially after making bone broth. Why? Because you can turn them into a wholesome homemade bone meal for your doggo'! Keep dry bones in a sealed container or freezer bag until you have enough for our special bone meal recipe.

Adding bone meal to your homemade dog food doesn't just make it tastier – it also packs a punch of calcium and helps reduce the harmful phosphorus buildup that can come with a high-meat diet. Your pup's health will thank you for it!

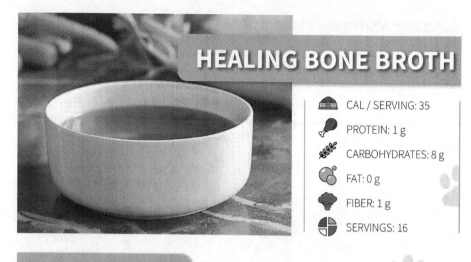

HEALING BONE BROTH

CAL / SERVING: 35

PROTEIN: 1 g

CARBOHYDRATES: 8 g

FAT: 0 g

FIBER: 1 g

SERVINGS: 16

INGREDIENTS

- ☐ 4 pounds of mixed bones *(chicken or turkey necks, feet, or knuckles - or beef marrow bones - are great, as they are rich in collagen)*
- ☐ 4 liters of water *(enough to cover the bones)*
- ☐ 2 tablespoons of apple cider vinegar *(helps in nutrient extraction)*

OPTIONAL INGREDIENTS FOR ADDED NUTRITION

- ☐ 1/2 cup of chopped carrots
- ☐ 1/2 cup of chopped parsley
- ☐ 1/2 cup chopped celery

DIRECTIONS

1) Prep the Bones:

If you use beef bones, try roasting them first to improve their flavor for picky eaters. Place them on a baking sheet and roast at 400°F for 30 minutes.

2) Start the Broth:

Place the bones in a large slow cooker. Add water until the bones are fully covered. Stir in the apple cider vinegar.

3) Slow Cook:

Cover, then set your slow cooker on low for 24 - 48 hours.

4) Strain and Cool:

Carefully strain the broth to remove all bone fragments and vegetables. Allow it to cool. As it cools, fat will solidify on the surface; skim this off and discard.

Discard any leftover bone broth about two hours after serving to avoid spoilage. After making bone broth, it typically cools and becomes jelly-like in consistency. Dilute concentrated broth for drinking and cooking by mixing ¼ cup of the concentrate with hot water until diluted, then adding to one gallon of drinking water.

CHEF'S TIP

7.2 Easy Bone Meal Recipe

Bone meal is a powerful way to provide essential calcium for your dog, putting you in control of their health. But remember, it's crucial to do it safely and correctly. Here are the steps to make bone meal for your dog:

Boil the Bones:

- Place the bones in a large pot and cover them with water.
- Bring the water to a boil and then reduce to a simmer.
- Simmer the bones for at least 12 hours. This helps to soften the bones and make them easier to grind.

Bake the Bones:

- Preheat your oven to 250°F (120°C).
- Remove the bones from the pot and place them on a baking sheet.
- Bake the bones in the oven for 2-3 hours until completely dry and brittle.

Grind the Bones:

- Once the bones are dry and brittle, let them cool.
- Grind the bones into a fine powder using a blender or food processor. Depending on your equipment size, you may need to do this in batches.

Chef Tips:

- Store the bone meal in an airtight container in a cool, dry place.
- **Dosage:** A general recommendation is to add about 1 teaspoon of bone meal per pound of homemade dog food. However, it's crucial to consult with a veterinarian to determine the correct amount for your dog's specific dietary needs.
- **Balanced Diet:** Ensure your dog gets a balanced diet with all necessary nutrients. Calcium is essential, but so are other vitamins and minerals. By providing a balanced diet, you are taking a proactive step in maintaining your dog's overall health.

- **Bone Safety:** Never feed cooked bones directly to your dog, as they can splinter and cause internal injuries. This safety precaution can ensure your dog's safety and prevent potential harm.

Following these steps and guidelines, you can safely make and use a homemade bone meal to supplement your dog's calcium intake.

7.2 Probiotic Fermented Vegetable Recipe

Creating probiotic-rich foods for dogs at home can be rewarding to support their digestive health and overall well-being. Fermented foods like homemade kefir and fermented vegetables are excellent sources of beneficial bacteria. Let us discover how to make a dog-friendly version of these probiotic powerhouses:

Nutritional Benefits:

Fermented vegetables are a great source of fiber and vitamins A, C, and K, depending on the vegetables used. Fermentation also produces beneficial probiotics that support gut health, improve digestion, and boost the immune system.

Don't let the idea of fermented anything put you off. This is a good thing for your pup.

PROBIOTIC
FERMENTED VEGETABLES

CAL / SERVING: 0

PROTEIN: 0 g

CARBOHYDRATES: 0 g

FAT: 0 g

FIBER: 0 g

SERVINGS: 4

INGREDIENTS

- [ ] 1 cup of dog-safe vegetables, finely chopped *(such as carrots, green beans, or broccoli)*
- [ ] 2 cups of water
- [ ] 1 tablespoon of sea salt

ALSO NEEDED

- [ ] A clean, glass jar
- [ ] Breathable fabric material *(such as clean, cotton cloth)*
- [ ] A rubber band

DIRECTIONS

1) Dissolve the salt in the water to make a brine.

2) Place the chopped vegetables in a clean glass jar.

3) Pour brine over the vegetables, ensuring they are completely submerged. Leave about an inch of space at the top.

4) Cover the jar with your breathable fabric, then secure it with the rubber band.

5) Let the jar sit at room temperature for 3 to 7 days. Check daily to ensure vegetables remain submerged, adding more brine if necessary.

6) Taste test the vegetables. Once fermented to your liking, replace the breathable cover with a tight lid and store it in the refrigerator.

Introduce Slowly: Start with small amounts to see how your dog reacts; every dog's digestive system is different.

Hygiene: Ensure all utensils, jars, and your working area are clean to avoid contamination.

Vegetable Choices: Only use dog-safe vegetables, and avoid those known to be toxic to dogs, such as onions and garlic.

Chapter 8:

EASY AND NUTRITIOUS STARTER RECIPES

In the soft glow of dawn, the kitchen becomes a space for meal preparation and a sanctuary where the bond between pet and owner strengthens with every chop, stir, and simmer. Here, amid the clatter of utensils and the aroma of fresh ingredients, creating meals for our canine friends transforms from a daily task into an expression of care. In this place of warmth and love, we begin our exploration of starter recipes designed not only to nourish but also to introduce seasoned chefs and novices to the joys and benefits of homemade dog food.

Consider waking up early to prepare a meal for your partner. The act of cooking not only nourishes their body but also strengthens your bond together. Now, imagine the same with your furry friend. The process of preparing their meal, the anticipation in their eyes, and the shared mealtime can deepen your connection and make you feel loved. So, why not make it a regular part of your routine?

8.1 Beginner's Meal: Chicken and Rice Delight

An Easy Digestion Balanced Meal of Versatility

If you switch your dog's food to homemade, it's essential to do it gradually so their stomach can get used to it. An excellent way to start is with chicken and rice. It's simple to make and easy on your dog's digestive system. Chicken provides protein without being too heavy, and rice is a gentle carbohydrate that gives energy without irritating.

The great thing about chicken and rice is that you can adjust it to your dog's taste and needs. You can add vegetables like carrots or peas for extra nutrients, or use pumpkin instead of rice if your dog needs a grain-free meal. If you feel like you need more liquid... introduce some of that bone broth as the liquid of choice.

Meal Preparation Tips

Preparing this meal and most meals in bulk saves time and ensures that a healthy, home-cooked option is always available. After cooking, portion the meal into daily servings, allowing them to cool before transferring them to storage containers. Label each container with the date of preparation, feeding the oldest meals first. For those with limited time during the week, dedicating a few hours on a weekend to meal prep can transform the daunting task of daily cooking into a manageable and enjoyable activity. A great strategy is to lay out about 14 freezer-safe stackable containers (for a whole batch) on the kitchen counter and simultaneously portion out all the food. This approach streamlines the feeding process and incorporates each meal with the intentionality and love that form the core of homemade dog food.

Another tip. If you do any bulk meal prep for yourself or your family, this is an excellent time to do the same for your dog. It won't take any more time in the long run of the day's activities, and you will have checked off an important piece of your week's work for your dog's well-being at the same time you do it for your own family.

This is one more solid reason to take this time and do this for our dogs.

Remember the story about my friend who started on homemade food with the three dogs? In the ensuing years until their passing… not one 'sick dog' dog vet visit or bill. SO, see that any way you want, saving time in your own life, saving the worry and concern when things go sideways, saving a few thousand dollars throughout a pup's life, or maybe even just knowing the increased chances of a healthy dog well into 'old age' is enough. You decide why, but doing it is likely to create the reason.

Chicken and rice delight stands out for its simplicity and nutritional value in the symphony of flavors and nutrients that compose homemade dog food. This beginner meal, embodying the principles of gentle digestion, balanced nutrition, and versatility, serves as an ideal starting point for those embarking on the path of homemade canine cuisine. Through thoughtful preparation and a willingness to adapt, dog owners can ensure this basic recipe evolves to meet their beloved companions' changing needs and tastes.

CHICKEN AND RICE DELIGHT
Beginner's Meal

CAL / SERVING: 300 - 350

PROTEIN: 26 g

CARBOHYDRATES: 30 g

FAT: 8 g

FIBER: 2 - 3 g

SERVINGS: 10

INGREDIENTS

- 1.5 cups brown rice *(a good source of carbohydrates and fiber)*

- 3 pounds chicken breast *(a lean protein source)*

- 1 tablespoon olive oil *(for healthy fats)*

- 3 cups chopped spinach *(rich in vitamins A and C, as well as iron)*

- 2 carrots, shredded *(for beta-carotene and fiber)*

- 1 zucchini, shredded *(adds vitamins and minerals)*

DIRECTIONS

1) Cook the Rice:

Rinse 1.5 cups of brown rice under cold water. In a saucepan, combine the rice and 3 cups of water. Boil, then cover and simmer for 45 minutes until rice is cooked and water is fully absorbed.

2) Prepare the Chicken:

While the rice cooks, cut 3 pounds of chicken breast into small pieces. Heat the olive oil in a large pot over medium heat, add the chicken, and then cook until no longer pink.

3) Add the Vegetables:

Add the spinach, carrots, and zucchini to the chicken; the residual heat will soften the veggies.

4) Mix All Ingredients:

Combine the cooked rice, chicken, and veggies in a large bowl. Stir well to ensure even distribution.

Allow the food to cool before serving it to your dog. The appropriate portion size depends on your dog's size, weight, and activity level. Typically, 1/2 to 1 cup of food per serving is suitable for a medium-sized dog, adjusted according to your dog's needs.

CHEF'S TIP

8.2 Beef and Pumpkin

The 'Beef and Pumpkin' recipe is a nutritious and well-balanced meal designed to provide your dog with many nutrients for optimal health. This wholesome dish features lean beef as the primary protein source, supporting muscle development and maintenance. Including fiber-rich vegetables adds variety to the meal and promotes digestive health and regularity. The star ingredient, pumpkin, is a nutrient-dense superfood packed with vitamins, minerals, and antioxidants that support overall well-being.

This 'Beef and Pumpkin' recipe offers a delicious and healthy option for your canine companion. By combining lean protein from beef, fiber-rich vegetables, and the nutritional powerhouse of pumpkin, this meal provides a balanced approach to your dog's dietary needs. However, it is always important to consult your veterinarian or a canine nutritionist before changing your dog's diet, especially if your furry friend has specific health requirements. With the right guidance and a carefully crafted recipe like this, you can feel confident in providing your dog with a tasty and nourishing meal that supports their overall health and happiness.

BEEF AND PUMPKIN

 CAL / SERVING: 250 - 300

 PROTEIN: 20 g

 CARBOHYDRATES: ~15 g

 FAT: 10 g

 FIBER: 3 - 4 g

 SERVINGS: 10

INGREDIENTS

- ☐ 1 cup cooked brown rice *(provides carbohydrates and fiber)*
- ☐ 2 pounds of lean, ground beef *(a rich source of protein and iron)*
- ☐ 1 tablespoon olive oil *(for healthy fats)*
- ☐ 1/2 cup peas *(frozen or fresh; offers vitamins and minerals)*
- ☐ 1/2 cup carrots, diced *(for beta-carotene and fiber)*
- ☐ 1.5 cups of pumpkin puree *(do not use pumpkin pie filling; pumpkin puree is rich in fiber and vitamins)*

DIRECTIONS

1) Cook the Rice:

Prepare 1 cup of cooked brown rice according to the package instructions. Set aside to cool.

2) Brown the Beef:

Heat olive oil in a large skillet over medium heat. Add the lean ground beef and cook until browned and no longer pink. Break up the meat with a spatula as it cooks to ensure even cooking.

3) Prepare the Vegetables:

While cooking the beef, steam or boil 1/2 cup of diced carrots and 1/2 cup of peas until tender. 5-7 minutes for steaming or 3-4 minutes for boiling.

4) Mix all Ingredients:

Combine the cooked beef, prepared rice, cooked vegetables, and 1.5 cups of pumpkin puree in a large mixing bowl. Mix well.

Allow the food to cool before serving it to your dog. The appropriate portion size depends on your dog's size, weight, and activity level. Typically, 1/2 to 1 cup of food per serving is suitable for a medium-sized dog, adjusted according to your dog's needs.

8.3 Turkey and Quinoa Mash-Up

Finding easy-to-make and nutritious meals for homemade dog food can be challenging. However, one dish that stands out is the turkey and quinoa mash-up, which combines simple cooking techniques with healthy ingredients to create a balanced meal.

Turkey is an excellent protein source, a major building block for muscle repair and growth in dogs of all ages. It's also a lean meat, making it a good choice for dogs that need to watch their fat intake. Using responsibly sourced turkey shows you care about the environment and animal welfare.

Quinoa is a superfood rich in nutrients like fiber, vitamins, and minerals. It's also a great source of protein, containing all nine essential amino acids, vital for dogs with sensitivities to familiar protein sources. Mixing quinoa with turkey adds texture and flavor to the dish, making it more appealing to your dog.

Preparing this meal is quick and easy, perfect for busy pet owners. Quinoa cooks in just a few minutes, and lean turkey takes a little time. You can make a big batch of the dish and store it for later, giving your dog fresh, homemade food without spending much time in the kitchen.

Remember to include leafy greens like kale and spinach in your dog's meal to give it an extra boost of nutrients and antioxidants.

The turkey and quinoa mash-up is a fantastic option for dog owners who want to serve healthy, mouth-watering meals that are easy to prepare.

TURKEY AND QUINOA MASH-UP

 CAL / SERVING: 220

 PROTEIN: 20 g

 CARBOHYDRATES: 15 g

 FAT: 9 g

 FIBER: 2.5 g

 SERVINGS: 6

INGREDIENTS

- ☐ 1 pound lean ground turkey *(a great source of protein)*
- ☐ 1 cup quinoa *(a gluten-free source of carbohydrates and fiber)*
- ☐ 1 tablespoon olive oil *(for healthy fats)*
- ☐ 2 cups chopped spinach *(for vitamins and iron)*
- ☐ 1 carrot, diced *(for fiber and vitamin A)*
- ☐ 1 zucchini, diced *(for vitamins and low-calorie hydration)*
- ☐ 1/2 cup peas *(frozen or fresh; for vitamins and fiber)*
- ☐ 4 cups of water

DIRECTIONS

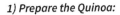

1) Prepare the Quinoa:

Rinse 1 cup of quinoa. In a saucepan, combine with 2 cups of water. Boil, cover, and simmer for about 15 minutes. Fluff and set aside to cool.

2) Cook the Turkey:

Heat 1 tablespoon of olive oil in a pan, then add the ground turkey. Cook until browned. Remove from heat and let cool.

3) Steam the Vegetables:

In a pot, steam chopped spinach, diced carrot, zucchini, and peas with 2 cups of water. Simmer, covered, for 5 - 7 minutes. Drain excess water.

4) Mix all Ingredients:

Combine the cooked quinoa, turkey, and vegetables in a large mixing bowl. Mix well.

5) Serve and Store:

Cool mixture before serving. A good starting point is about 1 cup of food per 20 pounds of body weight per day, divided into two meals. Store leftovers in the fridge for up to 5 days or freeze for up to 3 months.

 CHEF'S TIP

1) Use lean meats.
2) Add dog-safe veggies for variety.
3) Consider adding supplements under veterinary guidance for specific dietary needs.

8.4 Lamb and Greens

Lamb and Greens is a carefully designed recipe that delights your dog's palate and provides many health benefits. At the heart of this meal is lean lamb, an excellent source of protein that supports muscle maintenance and overall vitality. Including brown rice offers a healthy serving of carbohydrates for sustained energy, while its fiber content aids in maintaining digestive health. The true stars of this recipe are the dark leafy greens, such as spinach or kale, which are superfoods packed with vitamins A, C, E, and K. These nutrients work together to bolster immune health, enhance vision, and support proper cell function.

The 'Lamb and Greens' recipe harmoniously blends high-quality lamb protein, nutrient-dense dark leafy greens, and wholesome brown rice. A reasonable amount of coconut oil is incorporated to provide beneficial medium-chain fatty acids, which contribute to a glossy coat and healthy skin. This thoughtfully crafted meal goes beyond satisfying your dog's hunger; it aims to support optimal canine well-being by delivering a balanced and nutritious diet.

LAMB AND GREENS

 CAL / SERVING: 250

 PROTEIN: 18 g

 CARBOHYDRATES: 20 g

 FAT: 11 g

 FIBER: 3 g

 SERVINGS: 5

INGREDIENTS

- [ ] 1 pound ground lamb *(rich in protein and fatty acids)*
- [ ] 1 cup cooked brown rice *(provides carbohydrates and fiber)*
- [ ] 1 tablespoon coconut oil *(provides medium-chain fatty acids, which are beneficial for skin and coat health)*
- [ ] 2 cups dark leafy greens *(spinach or kale, chopped; excellent sources of vitamins A, C, E, and K)*
- [ ] 1/2 cup chopped parsley *(for fresh breath and additional vitamins)*
- [ ] 3 cups water

DIRECTIONS

1) Cook the Rice:

Rinse 1 cup of brown rice. In a saucepan, combine with 2 cups of water. Boil, cover, and simmer for about 45 minutes until tender. Set aside to cool.

2) Brown the Lamb:

Heat 1 tablespoon of coconut oil in a skillet over medium heat, then add the ground lamb. Cook until browned. Drain excess fat and let cool.

3) Prepare the Greens:

In a pot, steam dark leafy greens and parsley with 2 cups of water. Cover and steam for 5-7 minutes. Remove from heat and let cool.

4) Mix All Ingredients:

Combine the cooked rice, browned lamb, and steamed greens in a large mixing bowl. Mix well.

5) Serve and Store:

Cool mixture before serving. A good starting point is about 1 cup of food per 20 pounds of body weight per day, divided into two meals. Store leftovers in the fridge for up to 5 days or freeze for up to 3 months.

8.5 Fish Dish: Salmon and Sweet Potato

The 'Salmon and Sweet Potato' recipe is a delicious and healthy meal for your dog. It includes salmon, sweet potatoes, green beans, and blueberries, packed with nutrients that support your dog's heart, immune system, and skin and coat health.

This well-balanced dish combines multiple proteins, healthy fats, and vitamins, making it an excellent choice for your furry friend. Salmon's omega-3 fatty acids promote a shiny coat and healthy skin, while sweet potatoes provide fiber, vitamins, and minerals.

We speak of many of these dishes with these glowing benefits, and yes, each one truly is an excellent opportunity to advance your dog's health daily. That bouncy attitude, smile, bark, and a bit too quick consumption of the dish are all signs you are doing the right thing. Incorporating this meal into your dog's diet offers a flavorful and beneficial option they will love.

'Salmon and Sweet Potato' is a tasty and wholesome meal for your dog. The combination of nutrients in this dish contributes to your pet's overall well-being, with salmon providing essential omega-3 fatty acids for a healthy coat and skin and sweet potatoes offering fiber and vital vitamins and minerals. Treating your dog to this delightful recipe ensures they receive the nutrition they need to thrive while enjoying a flavorful meal.

Remember that when debating this or that on the menu, if you think, "MMMM, I would enjoy having this for dinner myself," you are likely on the right track for your pet.

SALMON AND SWEET POTATO
Fish Dish

CAL / SERVING: 280

PROTEIN: 23 g

CARBOHYDRATES: 22 g

FAT: 10 g

FIBER: 4 g

SERVINGS: 5 - 6

INGREDIENTS

- 1 pound salmon fillet *(skin removed, rich in omega-3 fatty acids for skin and coat health)*
- 2 medium sweet potatoes *(for fiber, vitamins A and C)*
- 1 tablespoon olive oil *(for healthy fats)*
- 1 cup chopped green beans *(for fiber, vitamins, and minerals)*
- 1/2 cup blueberries *(provides antioxidants for immune support)*
- 3 cups water

DIRECTIONS

1) Prepare the Sweet Potatoes:

Wash sweet potatoes, then poke holes in them with a fork. Boil or bake at 400°F for 45 - 50 minutes, until tender. Cool, peel, and mash.

2) Cook the Salmon:

Heat oven to 375°F. Brush salmon with olive oil and bake for 20 - 25 minutes until flaky. Cool, remove bones, and flake into small pieces.

3) Steam the Green Beans:

Trim and chop green beans. Steam for 5-7 minutes until tender but crisp. Cool.

4) Combine All Ingredients:

Mix mashed sweet potatoes, flaked salmon, steamed green beans, and blueberries in a bowl.

Bone Check: *Ensure all bones are removed from the salmon to prevent a choking hazard.*

Hydration: *Add water for additional hydration.*

Variety: *To add variety to your dog's diet, substitute green beans with other dog-safe vegetables, such as peas or carrots.*

Serving: *Feed 1 cup for every 20 pounds of body weight per day, split into two meals.*

8.6 Scrambled Eggs and Spinach

'Scrambled Eggs and Spinach Bliss' is a straightforward, nutritious meal designed with your dog's health in mind. Eggs provide a high-quality source of protein and essential amino acids for your dog's muscle health and cell repair, complemented by a suite of vitamins and minerals for comprehensive nutritional support. Spinach, rich in vitamins and antioxidants, aids in immune function and cellular health, while the added carrots contribute fiber and beta-carotene, promoting good vision and digestive health. Including cottage cheese adds a creamy texture and a calcium boost for solid bones and teeth. This recipe is perfect for dog owners looking to supplement their pet's diet with a protein-rich meal that supports overall health and vitality, minus grains. So, let's repeat: for pups with grain sensitivities, this is a fantastic meal on its own, and without the grain, makes it a superstar on your list!

Scrambled eggs and spinach makes a wholesome choice when preparing homemade dog food. These ingredients provide a simple yet nutritious option that nourishes your furry friend and helps strengthen the bond between you and your beloved pup. By opting for high-quality ingredients, you can guarantee that your dog begins its day with the promise of vitality and overall wellness without the risks of grain intolerance.

SCRAMBLED EGGS AND SPINACH

CAL / SERVING: 180

PROTEIN: 14 g

CARBOHYDRATES: 4 g

FAT: 12 g

FIBER: 1 g

SERVINGS: 4

INGREDIENTS

- [ ] 8 large eggs *(rich in protein and essential amino acids for muscle health and repair)*

- [ ] 1 tablespoon olive oil *(provides healthy fats for energy and vitamin E)*

- [ ] 2 cups fresh spinach *(packed with vitamins A, C, K, iron, and antioxidants)*

- [ ] 1/4 cup shredded carrots *(for fiber, beta-carotene, and natural sweetness)*

- [ ] 1/4 cup cottage cheese *(for calcium and protein)*

DIRECTIONS

1) Cook the Spinach:

Heat 1/2 tbsp olive oil in a skillet. Sauté spinach and shredded carrots until tender, about 3 - 4 minutes. Remove from heat and cool.

2) Scramble the Eggs:

Whisk eggs until beaten. Heat the remaining 1/2 tbsp olive oil in a skillet. Pour 8 large eggs into skillet and stir until set. Cook until fully cooked, but still moist.

3) Combine Ingredients:

Fold sautéed spinach, carrots, and cottage cheese into scrambled eggs evenly.

4) Mix All Ingredients:

Combine the cooked rice, chicken, and vegetables in a large bowl. Stir well to ensure even distribution.

5) Serve and Store:

Cool mixture before serving. A good starting point is about 1 cup of food per 20 pounds of body weight per day, divided into two meals. Store leftovers in the fridge for up to 5 days or freeze for up to 3 months.

8.7 Doggie Slow Cooker Stew

A slow cooker can be a great option if you're looking for an easy and healthy way to make meals for your dog. With this method, you can combine raw ingredients, such as beef and vegetables, and let them cook slowly over a few hours. The result is a delicious and nutritious stew your dog will love. It also takes some of the pressure of standing in the kitchen and watching paint dry while the food cooks. Set the cooker, move on to other items on your daily 'to-do' list, and return at the appropriate time, knowing 90% of your job is done.

Beef is an excellent protein source for building and repairing muscles and keeping skin and coat healthy. Vegetables, like sweet potatoes, carrots, and green beans, provide vitamins and minerals that support overall health. You can also use pumpkin or squash to add nutrients and support immune health and digestion.

The best part about this stew is that you can customize it based on your dog's needs and preferences. Depending on the season, you can use different vegetables or leave out ingredients if your dog has any sensitivities.

Cooking a big batch of stew has its advantages. One of them is that you can divide it into portions and freeze them for a later date. Stews can be helpful when you need a quick and easy meal for your dog. The best part is that reheating this homemade stew is easy and won't affect the quality of the food. Simmered in a pot, this Beef and Vegetable Stew is a great way to make homemade dog food. It ensures your dog gets a warm, healthy, and tasty meal that's easy to digest.

DOGGIE SLOW COOKER STEW

 CAL / SERVING: 250 - 300

 PROTEIN: 22 g

 CARBOHYDRATES: 20 g

 FAT: 8 g

 FIBER: 3 - 4 g

 SERVINGS: 10

INGREDIENTS

- ☐ 2 pounds lean beef chunks *(use cheaper cuts for stewing)*
- ☐ 2 chopped carrots *(for vitamins and fiber)*
- ☐ 1 cup chopped green beans *(provides extra vitamins, minerals, and fiber)*
- ☐ 1 cup cubed butternut squash *(for vitamins A and C)*
- ☐ 1/2 cup peas *(frozen or fresh; for vitamins and fiber)*
- ☐ 1.5 cups brown rice *(for healthy carbs and fiber)*
- ☐ 4 cups water

DIRECTIONS

1) Prepare the Ingredients:

Wash, then chop the carrots, green beans, and butternut squash into bite-sized pieces. Cut beef into chunks, if not pre-cut.

2) Combine in the Slow Cooker:

Place the beef, chopped vegetables, and brown rice in the slow cooker. Add 4 cups of water (or enough to cover the ingredients), then cover.

3) Cook:

Cook on low for 6 - 8 hours until meat is tender.

4) Cool and Serve:

Let stew cool before serving. Portion size depends on your dog's needs, but 1/2 to 1 cup per serving for medium-sized dogs is a good start.

Storage: Store in the fridge for up to 5 days or freeze in portion-sized containers for up to 3 months. Thaw in the fridge before serving.

Vegetable Variations: Add other dog-safe vegetables, such as sweet potatoes, zucchini, or spinach.

Grain-Free Option: Omit brown rice and add more vegetables, or try a grain-free alternative like diced apples (in moderation).

8.8 Help Make a Difference

Unlocking the Power of Generosity

"The greatest good you can do for another is not just to share your riches, but to reveal to him his own." - Benjamin Disraeli.

People who give without expectation live longer, happier lives and make more money. So if we've got a shot at that during our time together, darn it, I'm going to try.

To make that happen, I have a question: would you help someone you've never met, even if you never got credit for it?

Who is this person, you ask? They are like you—or, at least, like you used to be. They are less experienced, want to make a difference in their dog's life, and need help but are unsure where to look.

Our mission is to make homemade dog food accessible to everyone. Everything I do stems from that mission, and the only way to accomplish this is by reaching... well... everyone.

Your support is crucial. As it turns out, many individuals do judge a book by its cover (and its reviews). Therefore, I'm reaching out on behalf of a dog owner in need whom you may not know:

Please help that dog owner by leaving this book a review.

Your gift costs no money and takes less than 60 seconds to make, but it can change a fellow dog owner's life forever. Your review could help...

...one more dog enjoys a healthier, happier life.

...one more dog owner feels confident in providing for their fur babies.

...one more family deepens their bond with their canine companion.

...one more dog to experience the love and care they deserve.

...one more dream of a healthy, homemade dog diet has come true.

To get that 'feel good' feeling and help this person for real, all you have to do is...and it takes less than 60 seconds...

Leave a review!

I will thank you for it. Your pup will thank you for it.

Most of all, you will feel good for doing something for others in the same shoes you were in just a few weeks/months ago.

Scan the QR code below to leave your review:

www.amazon.com/review/review-your-purchases/?asin=B0DGQR27MP

If you feel good about helping a faceless dog owner, you are my kind of person. Welcome to the club. You're one of us!

I'm much more excited to help you create delicious, nutritious homemade meals for your dog faster, easier, and more joyfully than you can imagine. You'll love the recipes and tips I share in the coming chapters.

Thank you from the bottom of my heart. Now, back to our regularly scheduled programming.

- Your biggest fan, Chef John Wind.

PS - Fun fact: If you provide something of value to another person, it makes you more valuable to them. If you'd like goodwill straight from another dog owner - and believe this book will help them - send it their way.

Chapter 9:

NUTRIENT-SPECIFIC RECIPES FOR WELLNESS

"When feeding our dogs, it's important to ensure they receive all the necessary nutrition to stay healthy and happy. This section offers recipes specifically designed to meet their unique needs. By carefully selecting ingredients and creating well-balanced meals, these recipes are tasty and great for promoting optimal health."

9.1 Blood Health: Iron-Rich Liver and Lentils

The 'Iron-Rich Liver and Lentils' is a nutrient-dense meal designed to bolster your dog's health, mainly focusing on blood and iron levels. Beef liver, the star of this dish, is a powerhouse of nutrients, offering high-quality protein, Vitamin A, and an exceptional amount of iron, which is crucial for preventing anemia and supporting robust blood health. Adding green lentils contributes plant-based protein and fiber. It adds another layer of iron to the meal, ensuring your dog's energy levels remain steady. Kale introduces a wealth of vitamins and antioxidants, further enriching the meal with nutrients that support overall wellness. At the same time, diced apples provide a hint of sweetness and dietary fiber for digestive health.

When we cook meals, we usually focus on satisfying our hunger. But, by choosing ingredients rich in nutrients and good for our health, we can prepare meals that taste good and nourish our bodies. The 'Liver and Lentils' stands out in this regard. It combines various carefully chosen ingredients for health benefits, making a delicious and nutritious meal perfect for dogs.

And just because YOU don't eat or even like liver… is no excuse for not giving it to your four-legged partner. S/he will show you just how good it is. Maybe you too will begin to change your mind.

IRON-RICH LIVER AND LENTILS
Blood Health

 CAL / SERVING: 220

 PROTEIN: 20 g

 CARBOHYDRATES: 15 g

 FAT: 8 g

 FIBER: 3 g

 SERVINGS: 4

INGREDIENTS

- [ ] 1 pound beef liver or organ meat *(an excellent source of iron and vitamin A for supporting blood health and vision)*
- [ ] 1 cup green lentils *(rich in protein, fiber, and iron)*
- [ ] 1 tablespoon coconut oil *(for healthy fats)*
- [ ] 1/2 cup chopped kale *(for additional iron, vitamin C, minerals, and antioxidants)*
- [ ] 1/2 cup diced apples *(without the core and seeds; for fiber and natural sweetness)*
- [ ] 2 cups water

DIRECTIONS

1) Prepare the Lentils:

Rinse 1 cup of green lentils under cold water. In a saucepan, combine lentils with 2 cups of water. Boil, then simmer covered for 25-30 minutes until tender. Drain excess water and cool.

2) Cook the Liver:

Rinse beef liver under cold water and pat dry. Heat 1 tbsp coconut oil in a skillet over medium heat. Add liver to skillet and cook for 3-4 minutes on each side until no longer pink. Cool, then chop into small pieces.

3) Steam the Kale:

Rinse chopped kale and steam for about 5 minutes until slightly wilted. Cool.

4) Combine All Ingredients:

Gently mix all ingredients in a large bowl until well combined.

Cool the mixture completely before serving. Serving size ranges from 1/2 cup for small dogs to 1 1/2 cups for larger breeds, adjusted as needed. Refrigerate leftovers in an airtight container for up to 4 days, or freeze portions for up to 2 months, thawing as needed.

CHEF'S TIP

9.2 Calcium Boost: Sardine and Kale Stew

Calcium is essential for dogs to maintain strong bones, healthy teeth, and properly functioning muscles and heart. 'Sardine and Kale Stew' is a delicious and nutritious meal that provides an excellent source of calcium and other vital nutrients. Sardines with bones are rich in calcium, while kale offers a variety of vitamins and minerals, such as Vitamins A, C, and K, fiber, and beta-carotene. This well-balanced dish also contains protein and omega-3 fatty acids, contributing to your dog's overall health and well-being. Note: Don't let the bones put you off; they are soft and small enough not to be an issue for your fur baby.

Feeding your dog 'Sardine and Kale Stew' goes beyond providing the calcium they need for healthy bones and teeth. The nutrient-rich combination of sardines and kale supports your dog's health by promoting a shiny coat and a strong immune system. By incorporating this balanced and calcium-rich dish into your dog's diet, you can help ensure they receive the necessary nutrients to live a happy and healthy life.

SARDINE AND KALE STEW
Calcium Boost

 CAL / SERVING: 180

 PROTEIN: 20 g

 CARBOHYDRATES: 12 g

 FAT: 9 g

 FIBER: 3 g

 SERVINGS: 4

INGREDIENTS

- [ ] 1 cup of sardines in water *(for omega-3, protein, and calcium)*
- [ ] 1 cup chopped kale *(provides vitamins A, C, K, and calcium)*
- [ ] 1/2 cup diced sweet potatoes *(for carbs, fiber, and vitamins A and C)*
- [ ] 1 tbsp coconut oil *(for healthy fats; also aids digestion)*
- [ ] 1/4 cup chopped parsley *(freshens breath and provides vitamins)*
- [ ] 2 cups water *(or as needed for stew consistency)*

DIRECTIONS

1) Prepare the Sweet Potatoes:

Peel and dice sweet potatoes into small pieces. Boil until tender, about 10 - 15 minutes. Drain.

2) Cook the Kale:

Simmer chopped kale in 2 cups of water until tender, about 5 - 7 minutes.

3) Combine All Ingredients:

Add cooked sweet potatoes, sardines (with water for calcium), and coconut oil to the pot with kale. Stir gently. Heat over medium heat for 5 minutes, then stir in chopped parsley.

4) Serving and Storage:

Let stew cool to room temperature before serving. Feed 1/2 to 1 cup per 20 pounds daily. Leftovers can be stored in the fridge for up to 3 days or frozen for up to 2 months. Thaw as needed.

Calcium: *Use salt-free sardines in water for calcium.*

Variety: *To add variety to your dog's diet, swap in dog-safe veggies such as butternut squash or peas.*

By Age: *Puree for a smoother texture, suitable for puppies and seniors.*

9.3 Skin and Coat: Fish and Pumpkin Puree w/Flax Seed

Omega-3 fatty acids are essential building blocks for healthy cells in dogs. They are crucial in reducing inflammation, which can cause various health issues like skin problems and arthritis. Incorporating omega-3s into your pet's diet can help alleviate itchiness, hot spots, and other skin concerns while promoting a shiny, healthy coat. Additionally, omega-3s reduce pain and improve mobility in dogs suffering from arthritis.

Omega-Rich Fish and Pumpkin Puree is a delicious and nutrient-packed recipe designed to promote healthy skin and a lustrous coat in dogs. Salmon, the primary ingredient, provides a rich source of omega-3 fatty acids, while pumpkin puree adds fiber to support digestive health. Flaxseed oil further boosts the omega-3 and 6 fatty acid content, ensuring your dog receives a balanced blend of these necessary nutrients. Including spinach and blueberries elevates this meal to a powerhouse of antioxidants and vitamins, contributing to your dog's overall health and wellness. This recipe particularly benefits dogs needing extra skin and coat health support, those with arthritis, or those on the borderline of beginning arthritis.

FISH AND PUMPKIN PUREE
Skin and Coat

- CAL / SERVING: 250
- PROTEIN: 25 g
- CARBOHYDRATES: 10 g
- FAT: 13 g
- FIBER: 2 g
- SERVINGS: 3

INGREDIENTS

- ☐ 1 pound salmon or white fish *(rich in omega-3 fatty acids for skin and coat health)*
- ☐ 1 cup of pumpkin puree *(do not use pumpkin pie filling; pumpkin puree is rich in fiber and vitamins)*
- ☐ 1 tablespoon flaxseed oil *(for additional omega-3 and 6 fatty acids)*
- ☐ 1/2 cup chopped spinach *(for vitamins and minerals)*
- ☐ 1/4 cup blueberries *(provides antioxidants for overall health)*

DIRECTIONS

1) Cook the Fish:
Bake salmon or white fish at 375°F for 20 minutes until cooked. Remove bones, cool, and flake.

2) Prepare the Spinach:
Steam chopped spinach until wilted, about 3 - 5 minutes. Cool.

3) Mix All Ingredients:
Combine flaked fish, pumpkin puree, cooled spinach, and blueberries in a bowl. Drizzle with flaxseed oil and mix gently.

4) Serving and Storage:
Cool mixture to room temperature before serving. Adjust serving size based on your dog's needs. Refrigerate leftovers for up to 3 days or freeze for up to 2 months.

CHEF'S TIP

Bone Check: *Ensure all bones are removed from the fish to prevent a choking hazard.*

Freshness: *Use fresh, thoroughly-cooked fish to avoid parasites.*

Nutrition: *To provide extra nutrition, add in dog-safe, easily digestible veggies such as diced carrots or peas.*

9.4 Berry Antioxidant Boost Bowl

One way to ensure our dogs get all the proper nutrients is by giving them foods full of antioxidants. Berries are a fantastic source of antioxidants, and each type of berry contains unique vitamins and minerals that can help keep our dogs healthy. For example, blueberries can help keep the heart and brain healthy, while strawberries can boost the immune system and keep the skin healthy. Raspberries contain compounds that might help reduce the risk of cancer. Combining berries with lean proteins like chicken can provide a balanced and nutritious meal that helps with everything from muscle health to immune function.

There are many ways to give our dogs these healthy foods, such as blending berries into a sauce and pouring it over cooked chicken or freezing berry puree into treats for a refreshing snack. The Berry Antioxidant Boost Bowl is an excellent choice for a super-healthy meal that supports overall well-being and vitality. It contains mixed berries full of antioxidants, lean chicken for strong muscles, quinoa for good digestion, chia seeds for healthy skin, and Greek yogurt for a healthy gut.

BERRY ANTIOXIDANT BOOST BOWL

 CAL / SERVING: 260

 PROTEIN: 24 g

CARBOHYDRATES: 25 g

 FAT: 8 g

 FIBER: 5 g

 SERVINGS: 3

INGREDIENTS

- ☐ 1/2 pound lean chicken breast *(provides high-quality protein)*
- ☐ 1 cup mixed unsweetened berries *(blueberries, strawberries, raspberries; provides antioxidants for immune support)*
- ☐ 1/2 cup cooked quinoa *(for complete protein and fiber)*
- ☐ 1 tbsp chia seeds *(omega-3 for skin and coat health)*
- ☐ 1/2 cup steamed spinach *(for vitamins and minerals)*
- ☐ 2 tbsp plain Greek yogurt *(adds probiotics for digestive health)*

DIRECTIONS

1) Prepare the Chicken:

Boil the chicken breast in about one inch of water; then reduce heat, cover, and simmer for 16 minutes. Let it cool, then shred into bite-sized pieces.

2) Steam the Spinach:

Lightly steam spinach until wilted, about 2 - 3 minutes. Let cool.

3) Cook the Quinoa:

Rinse 1/2 cup quinoa under cold water. Combine quinoa with 1 cup water in a saucepan. Boil, then simmer covered for 15 minutes until water is absorbed. Fluff with a fork and cool.

4) Mix All Ingredients:

Combine chicken, cooled quinoa, steamed spinach, and mixed berries in a bowl. Gently toss.

5) Serve:

Before serving, top each portion with a sprinkle of chia seeds and a dollop of Greek yogurt.

Cool mixture to room temperature. Serve as a treat or supplement to your dog's diet. Adjust serving size based on your dog's needs. Store leftovers in the fridge for up to 2 days in an airtight container.

9.5 High-Energy Athletic Dog Fuel Recipe

For active dogs full of energy, it's important to consider feeding them a diet that suits their lifestyle. To keep up with their daily activities like running, jumping, and exploring, provide them with food that replenishes their energy and anticipates the demands on their active bodies. Creating meals that cater to their high-energy needs means maintaining a balance of macronutrients that support their vitality and promote their long-term health.

The key to this nutritionally dense food is carefully balancing calories, proteins, fats, and carbohydrates. Proper hydration is also crucial for our active dogs. By creating high-energy recipes that carefully balance calories, macronutrients, and hydration, we can provide our active dogs with the fuel they need to stay vibrant and healthy. Understanding their unique nutritional needs can nourish them with every bite and help them thrive.

HIGH-ENERGY
ATHLETIC DOG FUEL

 CAL / SERVING: 300

 PROTEIN: 25 g

 CARBOHYDRATES: 22 g

 FAT: 15 g

 FIBER: 3 g

 SERVINGS: 4

INGREDIENTS

- 1 pound lean ground beef *(muscle repair and energy)*
- 1 cup cooked brown rice *(provides complex carbs for sustained energy)*
- 1/2 cup mashed sweet potato *(beta-carotene and endurance vitamins)*
- 1/4 cup cooked oats *(fiber and slow-releasing energy)*
- 1 tbsp xylitol-free peanut butter *(for healthy fats)*
- 1/4 cup shredded carrots *(for fiber and vitamins)*
- 1 egg *(extra protein and essential fatty acids)*
- 2 tbsp crushed pumpkin seeds *(rich in zinc and antioxidants)*

DIRECTIONS

1) Cook the Rice and Oats:

Cook brown rice and oats separately according to package instructions. Set aside to cool.

2) Prepare the Sweet Potato:

Boil until soft or bake sweet potato for 45 - 60 minutes at 400°F. Cool, then peel and mash.

3) Cook the Beef:

Brown ground beef in a skillet over medium heat, breaking up to ensure even cooking. Drain excess fat.

4) Mix All Ingredients:

Combine cooked ground beef, cooled rice, oats, mashed sweet potato, shredded carrots, and peanut butter in a large bowl. Add egg and stir well.

5) Add the Pumpkin Seeds:

Sprinkle crushed pumpkin seeds into the mixture and stir.

Cool the mixture before serving. Adjust portions based on your dog's size and activity level. Store leftovers in the fridge for up to 4 days, or freeze for longer storage.

9.6 Immune-Boosting Chicken Soup

The Immune-Boosting Chicken Soup is a comforting and nourishing recipe designed to support your dog's immune system while providing a delicious and satisfying meal. This hearty soup features lean chicken as the primary protein source, offering amino acids crucial for maintaining muscle mass and overall health. The colorful medley of carrots, sweet potatoes, and kale infuses the dish with a powerful blend of Vitamins A, C, and K, which play vital roles in immune defense and general well-being. The addition of blueberries introduces a natural source of potent antioxidants, helping to protect against cellular damage and inflammation. Chicken soup is good for humans, so it has to be good for our dogs!

This Immune-Boosting Chicken Soup is a comfort food that will warm your dog's heart and a nutrient-rich option tailored to support their immune system. By combining lean chicken, a vibrant mix of vegetables, and the immune-boosting properties of blueberries and turmeric, this recipe provides a comprehensive approach to your dog's health. Turmeric, renowned for its anti-inflammatory qualities, offers an extra layer of protection, promoting a healthy immune response. With this nourishing and flavorful soup, you can ensure your furry friend remains healthy, happy, and ready to tackle their daily adventures with a strong and resilient immune system.

IMMUNE-BOOSTING CHICKEN SOUP

 CAL / SERVING: 220

 PROTEIN: 26 g

CARBOHYDRATES: 18 g

 FAT: 3 g

 FIBER: 4 g

 SERVINGS: 11 - 12

INGREDIENTS

- [ ] 1 pound chicken breast *(protein to support muscles and immune system)*
- [ ] 1 cup diced carrots *(for beta-carotene and vitamins)*
- [ ] 1/2 cup chopped kale *(for vitamins and antioxidants)*
- [ ] 1/2 cup diced sweet potatoes *(for vitamins and immune support)*
- [ ] 1/4 cup blueberries *(rich in antioxidants)*
- [ ] 1 tbsp turmeric *(anti-inflammatory)*
- [ ] 4 cups unconcentrated bone broth *(gut health)*
- [ ] 2 tbsp chopped parsley *(for fresh breath and vitamins)*

DIRECTIONS

1) Prepare the Chicken:

Boil chicken breast in bone broth until fully cooked, about 15 - 20 minutes. Remove, cool, and then shred.

2) Cook the Vegetables:

In the same broth, simmer diced carrots and sweet potatoes until soft, about 10 minutes.

3) Add Kale and Blueberries:

Add chopped kale and blueberries, then simmer 5 more minutes until tender.

4) Season the Soup:

Stir in turmeric, add shredded chicken, then heat through for 5 minutes. Just before serving, stir in chopped parsley.

5) Serving and Storage:

Serve warm, ensuring it's not too hot for your dog. Store leftovers in the fridge for up to 3 days or freeze in portion-sized containers for up to 2 months.

CHEF'S TIP

Substitute Water: *If you don't have bone broth, don't worry; use water instead. As the ingredients cook, it will make its own broth.*
Seasoning: *Turmeric is potent, so use it sparingly.*
Variety: *Adjust the veggies to suit your dog's taste.*

Chapter 10:

SPECIAL NEED CONSIDERATIONS: ALLERGIES, SENSITIVITIES, AND SUPPLEMENTS

When it comes to feeding our dogs, it's important to recognize their dietary needs, which may include special considerations for allergies, sensitivities, and health conditions. Admittedly, this is the same as if we had allergies or health conditions dealing with foods. As loving pet owners, we must tailor our meal preparations to address these individual requirements. This chapter explores the importance of creating hypoallergenic options, meals for sensitive stomachs, and condition-specific recipes to ensure the health and happiness of our fur babies. We should look after ourselves with this level of concern and detail when planning meals.

Conditions

When it comes to feeding dogs, it's about more than just giving them essential nutrients. Dog owners must be careful when preparing meals for their pets and consider their individual needs. It's a way of showing love and dedication to their furry companions.

Sensitive Stomachs

Selecting ingredients that are easy to digest becomes important for dogs whose digestive systems demand a gentler approach. Meals designed for sensitive stomachs prioritize simplicity and digestibility, incorporating ingredients soothing to the gut and conducive to optimal nutrient absorption. Boiling skinless white meat poultry or low-fat cottage cheese as protein sources and well-cooked, easily digestible carbohydrates such as white rice or pumpkin create a foundation for meals that support digestive health. The emphasis on minimal seasoning and avoiding fats and oils underscores the commitment to providing nourishment that respects the delicate balance of a sensitive digestive system.

Condition-Specific Meals

Addressing the dietary needs of dogs contending with specific health conditions such as kidney or heart disease requires collaboration between pet owners and veterinary professionals. This partnership, rooted in a shared goal of enhancing the dog's quality of life, guides the customization of recipes to support health and mitigate the impact of disease. For dogs with kidney disease, reducing phosphorus and protein in the diet and increasing omega-3 fatty acids can help manage the condition, necessitating careful selection of ingredients that align with these dietary goals. Similarly, dogs with heart disease benefit from meals low in sodium and rich in taurine and L-carnitine, necessitating a diet that supports cardiac function without exacerbating the condition. The crafting of these meals, inherently personalized, reflects a deep commitment to the health and well-being of dogs, ensuring each dish serves as a vehicle for healing and comfort.

Supplement Integration

Supplements like fish oil, probiotics, and glucosamine can be added to a dog's diet to address deficiencies or support specific health conditions. By integrating these supplements thoughtfully, pet owners can create customized nutrition tailored to their dog's needs. This approach ensures that dogs receive the critical nutrients they require for overall health.

10.1 Special Diet Recipes - Puppies Power Bowl

Puppies have unique nutritional requirements to support their rapid growth and development. The Puppy Power Bowl is a carefully crafted recipe that meets these needs, providing a balanced blend of essential nutrients. This wholesome meal features lean ground turkey as a high-quality protein source, promoting muscle growth and repair. Brown rice and pumpkin puree offer easily digestible carbohydrates and fiber, supporting healthy digestion and providing the energy needed for active puppies. Including flaxseed oil ensures an adequate supply of omega-3 fatty acids for cognitive development and maintaining a healthy coat.

The Puppy Power Bowl is a nutritionally complete recipe designed to support the overall development of growing puppies. This balanced meal provides essential building blocks for healthy growth, including high-quality protein from lean ground turkey, digestible carbohydrates, fiber from brown rice and pumpkin puree, and omega-3 fatty acids from flaxseed oil. Cottage cheese adds a valuable calcium boost, promoting strong bone development. By offering this wholesome foundation, this meal contributes to puppies' proper growth, energy levels, and overall health during their critical early life stages.

PUPPIES POWER BOWL

CAL / SERVING: 300

PROTEIN: 24 g

CARBOHYDRATES: 20 g

FAT: 12 g

FIBER: 3 g

SERVINGS: 6

INGREDIENTS

- ☐ 1 pound ground turkey *(protein for muscle growth)*
- ☐ 1 cup cooked brown rice *(carbohydrates for energy)*
- ☐ 1/2 cup carrots, finely grated *(vitamins and minerals for development)*
- ☐ 1/4 cup peas *(provides fiber and protein)*
- ☐ 1/4 cup pumpkin puree *(not pie filling; for digestive health and fiber)*
- ☐ 1 tablespoon flaxseed oil *(omega-3 fatty acids for brain development)*
- ☐ 1/4 cup cottage cheese *(calcium for bone growth)*

DIRECTIONS

1) Cook the Turkey and Rice:

Cook turkey in a skillet over medium heat until fully cooked, breaking it into small pieces. Drain excess fat. Prepare brown rice according to package instructions. Let cool.

2) Prepare the Vegetables:

Steam or boil carrots and peas until soft. Let cool.

3) Combine the Ingredients:

Mix turkey, rice, carrots, peas, and pumpkin puree in a large bowl. Ensure even distribution.

4) Add the Supplements:

Drizzle flaxseed oil over the mixture and add cottage cheese. Stir well to incorporate.

5) Serving and Storage:

Cool before serving. Puppy portions vary; start with small, frequent meals. Store leftovers in the fridge for up to 3 days or freeze for up to 2 months.

CHEF'S TIP

Cooking Method: Remember, steaming is always preferable to boiling for nutrient retention, especially for puppies.

Portioning: Adjust portions based on the puppy's breed, size, and age. Start with 1/4 to 1 cup spread over 3 - 4 meals daily.

10.2 Gentle Balance Senior Dog Meal

As dogs enter their golden years, their nutritional needs change, requiring a diet focusing on easy digestion, joint health, and maintaining cognitive function. The Gentle Balance Senior Dog Meal is a recipe crafted for these needs. Lean ground chicken and oatmeal form the foundation of this protein-rich yet easily digestible meal, ensuring senior dogs receive the nutrients they need without putting undue stress on their digestive system. Blueberries are included for their potent antioxidant benefits, helping to support aging cells and overall health.

The Gentle Balance Senior Dog Meal prioritizes easy digestion with lean ground chicken and oatmeal while incorporating ingredients supporting joint health and cognitive function, such as flaxseed, which provides essential omega-3 fatty acids to reduce inflammation. Pumpkin and green beans are thoughtfully chosen for their fiber content and low caloric density, helping senior dogs maintain a healthy weight without compromising nutrient intake. By offering a well-rounded meal tailored to the specific requirements of older dogs, the Gentle Balance Senior Dog Meal aims to keep them healthy, happy, and thriving throughout their golden years.

GENTLE BALANCE MEAL
For Senior Dogs

 CAL / SERVING: 250

 PROTEIN: 15 g

CARBOHYDRATES: 23 g

 FAT: 9 g

FIBER: 3 g

 SERVINGS: 6

INGREDIENTS

- ☐ 1 pound ground chicken *(easy to digest and low in fat)*
- ☐ 1 cup cooked oatmeal *(soluble fiber and a stable energy source)*
- ☐ 1/2 cup blueberries *(rich in antioxidants and for cognitive health)*
- ☐ 1/4 cup green beans *(a low-calorie source of vitamins)*
- ☐ 1/4 cup pumpkin *(provides fiber for digestion)*
- ☐ 2 tbsp ground flaxseed *(for omega-3 fatty acids and joint health)*
- ☐ Supplements: See recipe notes

DIRECTIONS

1) Prepare the Chicken:

Cook ground chicken in a pan over medium heat until fully cooked. Let it cool.

2) Cook the Oatmeal:

Prepare oatmeal per package instructions using water or bone broth. Ensure it's cooled.

3) Prepare the Vegetables:

Steam green beans and pumpkin until tender. Mash the pumpkin once cooled.

4) Mix All Ingredients:

Combine chicken, oatmeal, mashed pumpkin, steamed green beans, and blueberries. Mix well.

5) Supplements:

Mix in supplements like glucosamine or omega-3s as per your vet's recommendation.

Serving: *Serve at room temperature. Portion sizes vary by dog size. Refrigerate leftovers for up to 3 days or freeze.*

Hydration: *Add bone broth to prevent dehydration in seniors.*

Consistency: *Puree meals for dogs with dental issues.*

10.3 Hypoallergenic Fish and Pea Recipe:

Dogs with food sensitivities require a carefully crafted diet to minimize the risk of allergic reactions while providing essential nutrients for optimal health. The Hypoallergenic Fish & Pea Delight is a gentle and nutritious meal designed to meet these needs. This recipe features whitefish as a highly digestible source of lean protein, crucial for maintaining muscle health without the common allergens found in poultry or beef. Green peas are a grain-free source of fiber and additional protein, supporting digestive health and overall well-being.

The Hypoallergenic Fish & Pea Delight is a thoughtfully crafted meal for dogs with food sensitivities, offering a balance of flavors and nutrients without common allergens. Whitefish provides a gentle, lean protein source, while green peas and sweet potatoes contribute grain-free fiber, vitamins, and minerals to support digestive health and overall well-being. The addition of olive oil promotes a shiny coat and healthy skin through the inclusion of healthy fats. Parsley freshens breath and offers antioxidants to support the immune system. This hypoallergenic recipe is ideal for pet owners looking to nourish their dogs with sensitivities, ensuring they receive the necessary nutrients for optimal health while minimizing the risk of allergic reactions.

HYPOALLERGENIC FISH AND PEA

CAL / SERVING: 200

PROTEIN: 20 g

CARBOHYDRATES: 15 g

FAT: 6 g

FIBER: 3 g

SERVINGS: 6

INGREDIENTS

- [ ] 1 pound suitable white fish, such as haddock *(for easily-digestible, lean protein)*
- [ ] 1 cup green peas *(fiber-rich, grain-free protein)*
- [ ] 1 sweet potato *(provides fiber and vitamins)*
- [ ] 1 tbsp olive oil *(for skin and coat health)*
- [ ] 1/4 cup parsley *(freshens breath and adds vitamins)*

DIRECTIONS

1) Prepare the Fish:

Bake or steam until flaky. Debone, cool, and flake.

2) Cook the Sweet Potato and Peas:

Boil or bake the sweet potato until tender, then mash. Cook peas until tender, then cool.

3) Mix All Ingredients:

Combine fish, mashed sweet potato, and peas. Drizzle with olive oil and mix.

4) Add the Parsley:

Fold in chopped parsley for flavor and nutrition.

5) Serving and Storage:

Cool before serving. Adjust portions as needed. Store in fridge for 3 days or freeze for 2 months.

Bone Check: *Ensure all bones are removed from the fish to prevent a choking hazard.*

Ingredient Selection: *Avoid canned peas with added sodium and introduce the peas gradually. Look for high-quality olive oil.*

Variety: *For variety, try sardines, venison, duck, or kangaroo.*

Grain-Free: *Opt for grain-free carbs, such as sweet potatoes.*

CHEF'S TIP

10.4 Grain-Free Chicken & Veggie Medley

Finding a balanced and nutritious diet can be challenging for dogs with grain sensitivities or allergies. The 'Grain-Free Chicken & Veggie Medley' is designed to meet this need, providing a wholesome meal that excludes grains while offering essential nutrients for overall health. This recipe features high-quality lean protein from ground chicken and a medley of vegetables that provide fiber, vitamins, and minerals. Including coconut oil and flaxseed ensures a supply of healthy fats, particularly omega-3 fatty acids, known for their anti-inflammatory properties and ability to support skin, coat, and brain health.

The 'Grain-Free Chicken & Veggie Medley' is a nutrient-dense meal designed to support the vitality and well-being of dogs on a grain-free diet. This recipe combines lean ground chicken with various vegetables, providing essential protein, fiber, vitamins, and minerals. Adding coconut oil and flaxseed offers a source of healthy fats, including omega-3 fatty acids, which help reduce inflammation, promote skin and coat health, and support optimal brain function. Blueberries are included as a delicious source of antioxidants, contributing to immune health and disease prevention. By offering a balanced, grain-free option, this meal ensures that dogs with grain sensitivities or allergies can still receive the nutrition they need to thrive.

CHICKEN AND VEGGIE MEDLEY
Grain-Free

CAL / SERVING: 220

PROTEIN: 24 g

CARBOHYDRATES: 8 g

FAT: 10 g

FIBER: 3 g

SERVINGS: 6

INGREDIENTS

- 1 pound ground chicken *(lean protein for muscle maintenance)*
- 1/2 cup mashed pumpkin *(fiber-rich and grain-free)*
- 1/4 cup chopped spinach *(vitamins A and C, plus iron)*
- 1/4 cup chopped zucchini *(a low-calorie source of vitamins and minerals)*
- 1 tbsp coconut oil *(healthy fats for skin and coat)*
- 2 tbsp ground flaxseed *(provides omega-3s and is anti-inflammatory)*
- 1/2 cup blueberries *(for antioxidants and immune support)*

DIRECTIONS

1) Cook the Chicken:

Brown and fully cook the ground chicken in a skillet over medium heat. Let it cool.

2) Prepare the Vegetables:

Steam the spinach and zucchini until tender. Let them cool.

3) Mix All Ingredients:

Mix cooled chicken, mashed pumpkin, spinach, zucchini, and blueberries evenly in a bowl.

4) Add Fats and Fiber:

Incorporate coconut oil and ground flaxseed for extra benefits.

Allow the food to cool before serving it to your dog. The appropriate portion size depends on your dog's size, weight, and activity level. Store leftovers in the fridge for up to 3 days or freeze for up to 2 months.

CHEF'S TIP

10.5 Digestive Health Booster Recipe:

The Digestive Health Booster Recipe is a carefully crafted meal designed to support your dog's digestive well-being. This recipe features lean ground turkey as the primary protein source, which is easy to digest and helps maintain muscle mass without overburdening the digestive system. Pumpkin, a well-known remedy for digestive issues in dogs, is a key ingredient in this recipe. It contains both soluble and insoluble fiber, promoting regular bowel movements and a healthy gut. Oatmeal, another excellent source of fiber, is included to support a balanced microbiome in the digestive tract.

This Digestive Health Booster Recipe is a nutritious and thoughtful approach to supporting your dog's digestive health. This meal combines easily digestible protein, fiber, and natural stomach-soothing properties by incorporating lean ground turkey, pumpkin, oatmeal, and ginger. Adding fermented vegetables or yogurt containing probiotics introduces beneficial bacteria that further aid digestion and boost the immune system. With this recipe, you can feel confident you are providing your furry friend with a balanced and nourishing meal that promotes optimal digestive health, ensuring they remain comfortable, happy, and ready to enjoy life to the fullest.

DIGESTIVE HEALTH BOOSTER

CAL / SERVING: 230

PROTEIN: 26 g

CARBOHYDRATES: 16 g

FAT: 7 g

FIBER: 3 g

SERVINGS: 6

INGREDIENTS

- ☐ 1 pound lean ground turkey *(high in protein and easy to digest)*
- ☐ 1 cup cooked pumpkin *(fiber-rich and aids digestion)*
- ☐ 1/2 cup cooked oats *(soluble fiber for gut health)*
- ☐ 1/4 cup fermented vegetables or low-fat yogurt *(probiotics for gut flora)*
- ☐ 1 tbsp grated ginger *(natural anti-inflammatory)*
- ☐ 1 tbsp chopped parsley per serving *(for fresh breath and added nutrients)*

DIRECTIONS

1) Prepare the Turkey:

Brown ground turkey in a skillet over medium heat until fully cooked. Ensure thorough cooking for easier digestion. Let it cool.

2) Cook the Pumpkin and Oats:

Cook the pumpkin until soft, mash, and let cool. Cook oats according to package instructions and cool. Canned pumpkin (pure, not pie filling) is convenient.

3) Combine All Ingredients:

In a large bowl, mix cooled ground turkey, pumpkin, oats, and grated ginger.

4) Add the Probiotics:

Stir in fermented vegetables or yogurt to maintain the probiotics' benefits.

Garnish with chopped parsley before serving; it aids digestion and freshens breath.

Ginger Caution: While ginger is beneficial, it should be used sparingly, especially for small dogs. Always start with a small amount to ensure it agrees with your dog's stomach.
Serving / Storage: Serve at room temperature; adjust portions based on size, age, and activity level. Store leftovers in an airtight container in the fridge for up to 3 days or freeze for up to 2 months.

Chapter 11:

DIET AND EXERCISE

In the early morning's still and peaceful hours, people and their pets form an unbreakable bond while sharing the quiet anticipation of the day ahead. This time of day offers the perfect opportunity to discuss the crucial roles of diet and exercise in maintaining a dog's health. The morning's tranquility sets the foundation for vitality, supporting the physical body and the spirit of our beloved canine friends.

11.1 Exercise and Diet: The Dynamic Duo

Activity Needs

A dog's diet should match its energy levels and daily activities. For example, a high-energy dog breed that spends most of its day running and playing requires a diet rich in proteins and fats to rebuild muscles and provide quick energy. On the other hand, older dogs who are less active need a diet that is lower in calories but rich in nutrients to support their joints and brain function.

Finding the right balance between diet and exercise can ensure your dog gets the necessary fuel to stay healthy and active. For instance, you can prepare a nutrient-packed breakfast before a morning hike to sustain your dog's muscles and endurance throughout the climb. A meal like lean chicken and oatmeal can be an excellent example of a balanced diet.

Post-Exercise Nutrition

After exertion, a dog's body enters a phase of recovery, a process supported by post-exercise nutrition. This meal, ideally rich in proteins and complex carbohydrates, aids in repairing muscle tissue and replenishing glycogen stores. A simple meal of fish, rich in omega-3 fatty acids, and apples or sweet potatoes offers a delicious end to a workout and a foundation for optimal recovery. This attention to post-exercise nutrition ensures a dog's body has the resources to repair and strengthen, preparing them for the next adventure.

Weight Management

The synergy of diet and exercise plays a pivotal role in managing a dog's weight, a balance that prevents the extremes of under or overweight, both harbingers of health issues. Regular, tailored exercise, complemented by a diet calibrated to the dog's caloric needs, ensures a healthy weight, supporting longevity and reducing the risk of diabetes and joint problems. This management, akin to a gardener tending to their plants, requires regular attention and adjustments, ensuring that a dog's weight remains within a healthy range.

Important note… just as people tend to overemphasize their weight and when on a diet, they weigh themselves five times a day and measure every ounce of food… we know this is going a little overboard; we need to maintain calm when dealing with our pups and realize that a day or two up or down isn't critical…but the direction over the course of a week or two weeks is more important. Check with your vet; they will advise you on how often to weigh and when to get concerned about ups and downs.

Exercise Variety

Just as a varied diet supports nutritional health, a diverse exercise routine prevents boredom, encouraging a dog to remain active and engaged. Alternating between walks, runs, agility training, and play sessions keeps a dog physically stimulated and mentally sharp. This variety, reflecting the multifaceted nature of canine health, ensures that exercise remains a joyous part of their daily routine, bonding, and exploration that complements the nutritional care provided through their diet.

11.2 The Role of Hydration in Your Dog's Diet

When it comes to taking care of dogs, it's essential to ensure they drink enough water. To help your dog drink more water, you can put bowls in different places around your home and ensure the water is always fresh. You can also use a water fountain, which might interest your dog and encourage her/him to drink more. Remember, keeping your dog hydrated is critical to keeping them healthy and happy!

Monitoring Hydration

To keep your dog hydrated, look for signs like moist gums, elastic skin, and bright eyes. You can also check their urine output for frequency and color. Provide multiple water stations and incorporate hydrating foods like watermelon and cucumbers into their meals.

Summer Strategies

As the summer heats up and the days get longer, we must ensure dogs stay hydrated. We can provide shaded spots for them to rest, cool down, and keep a bowl of fresh water nearby. Adding ice cubes to their water or freezing treats with fruit or bone broth can make staying hydrated fun and refreshing. And when we're out and about with our pups, it's essential to bring a portable water container to ensure they have access to water at all times. At the end of this chapter, we will cover a frozen treat recipe for summer fun!

11.3 Mental Stimulation and Diet: The Connection

Brain Foods

Including certain foods in a dog's diet can help improve their cognitive function, mental agility, and physical health. The latest research in canine nutrition backs this approach and involves choosing ingredients known to boost brain power. For example, fatty acids in fish like salmon and sardines are essential for brain function and activity. At the same time, antioxidants in berries and leafy greens can protect against damage to brain cells. Vitamins found in whole grains and lean meats also play a critical role in energy metabolism in the brain, which can support learning and mood regulation.

Feeding Games

I love feeding games for Dot! They are a great way to combine nutrition and mental stimulation by invoking their innate foraging instincts. Puzzle feeders and hiding food can challenge your dog's problem-solving skills and encourage physical and psychological engagement. Watching my dog Dot figure out these puzzles is an exciting and satisfying experience that never gets old. It's a great way to transform mundane necessities into exciting and fulfilling events while strengthening our bond. It also pushes the pup's ability to think through situations and come up with real answers, which is a solid way to help improve your dog's capacity for learning.

Diet Variety

Feeding your dog the same food can become dull and lead to a loss of interest in their meals. Introducing a variety of proteins, textures, fruits, and vegetables into their diet can keep their senses engaged and make mealtime more enjoyable for them. Additionally, giving your dog different foods requires them to be adaptable and resilient, which is good for their mental well-being.

11.4 Homemade Treats for Training and Bonding

For dog owners who love their dogs, homemade treats are a great way to show compassion. For example, some people make soft treats with pumpkin and oats or cook crispy chicken strips without harmful additives. These Peanut Butter Pumpkin Treats are also great for dog training and rewards for good behavior.

Homemade dog treats are a wonderful way for pet owners to show their love and compassion for their furry friends. These treats provide a delicious and healthy alternative to store-bought options and an opportunity for bonding and training. Dog owners can ensure their pets receive nutritious snacks by creating soft treats with wholesome ingredients like pumpkin and oats or cooking crispy chicken strips without harmful additives. Homemade treats are perfect for rewarding good behavior and can be essential in dog training.

11.5 Peanut Butter Pumpkin Treats

The 'Peanut Butter Pumpkin Treats' recipe is an easy-to-follow and nutritious option for dog owners looking to create homemade treats. These tasty treats will surely be a hit with your dog, and they contain healthy ingredients that can benefit your pet's overall well-being. However, it's essential to remember if your dog has any specific dietary needs or restrictions, it's always best to consult your veterinarian before introducing any changes to their diet or treats. Creating homemade treats provides your dog with a delicious and healthy snack and strengthens the bond between you and your beloved companion.

PEANUT BUTTER
PUMPKIN TREATS

 CAL / SERVING: 30 - 40

 PROTEIN: 1 g

 CARBOHYDRATES: 8.9 g

 FAT: 2.5 g

 FIBER: 0.8 g

 SERVINGS: 25 - 30

INGREDIENTS

- 2- 1/2 cups whole wheat flour *(or use oat flour for gluten-free)*
- 2 eggs
- 1/2 cup of pumpkin puree *(do not use pumpkin pie filling; pumpkin puree is rich in fiber and vitamins)*
- 2 tablespoons xylitol-free peanut butter *(for healthy fats)*
- 1/2 teaspoon ground cinnamon

DIRECTIONS

1) Preheat oven to 350°F (175°C).

2) Mix dry ingredients (flour and cinnamon) in a large bowl.

3) Add eggs, pumpkin, and peanut butter, then stir into dough. Adjust consistency if needed.

4) Knead dough on a floured surface until smooth.

5) Roll out dough to 1/2 inch thickness; cut treats with a cookie cutter or knife.

6) Place treats on a parchment-lined baking sheet.

7) Bake for 25 - 30 minutes until golden and firm. Cool on a wire rack before serving.

Store in an airtight container for up to a month or freeze for longer.

Safety: *Check peanut butter for xylitol, which is toxic to dogs.*
Substitute Flour: *Use oat or coconut flour for wheat-sensitive dogs.*
Recipe Adjustments: *Adjust treat thickness for chewiness preference. For softer treats, add more pumpkin or reduce baking time.*
Mix It Up: *Customize with dog-safe extras like carrots or apples.*

11.6 Summer Breeze Frozen Treats

Beat the heat and pamper your furry friend with these delightful Summer Breeze Frozen Yogurt Treats. These treats are designed to keep your dog cool and hydrated during the warmer months and are a perfect blend of nutrition and indulgence. The creamy base of Greek yogurt provides a luscious texture and delivers a healthy dose of probiotics to support digestive health and protein for maintaining strong muscles. Adding blueberries, strawberries, and bananas infuses these treats with natural sweetness and flavor while supplying essential vitamins, antioxidants, and fiber that contribute to overall health and immune function.

These 'Summer Breeze Frozen Yogurt Treats' are a simple and fun way to show your dog extra love and care during the hot summer months. Combining the nutritional benefits of Greek yogurt, blueberries, strawberries, and bananas, these frozen delights offer a refreshing and healthy snack that keeps your puppers cool, satisfied, and nourished. Always choose plain, unsweetened varieties of yogurt and fruits to ensure the treats are safe and appropriate for your dog's dietary needs. With these easy-to-make frozen yogurt treats, you can provide your furry companion with a delicious and wholesome way to beat the heat and enjoy a tasty, health-promoting indulgence.

SUMMER BREEZE FROZEN TREATS

CAL / SERVING: 45

PROTEIN: 2 g

CARBOHYDRATES: 6 g

FAT: 0.5 g

FIBER: 0.5 g

SERVINGS: 20

INGREDIENTS

- [ ] 2 cups plain Greek yogurt *(high in protein, as well as probiotics for digestive health)*
- [ ] 1/2 cup blueberries *(rich in antioxidants for immune support)*
- [ ] 1/2 cup strawberries, chopped *(provides vitamins A and C for overall health)*
- [ ] 1 banana, mashed *(for potassium and fiber)*
- [ ] 2 tablespoons honey *(for natural sweetness - optional)*

ALSO NEEDED

- [ ] Silicone ice cube trays, small dog treat molds, or a plastic ice cube tray

DIRECTIONS

1) Mix All Ingredients:

In a large bowl, mix plain Greek yogurt, mashed banana, blueberries, strawberries, and honey (if you like). Stir well.

2) Prepare the Molds:

Spoon the mix into silicone ice cube trays or small dog treat molds. If you don't have molds, use an ice cube tray.

3) Freeze:

Put the filled molds or trays in the freezer. Freeze for at least 4 hours until solid.

4) Serve:

Once frozen, pop the treats out of the molds. Let your dog enjoy a cool treat on hot days.

5) Storage:

Keep any leftovers in an airtight container or zip-lock bag in the freezer for up to 3 months.

Fruit Variations: For variety, feel free to substitute or add other dog-safe fruits, such as peeled apple pieces or melons.

11.7 Beginner's Guide to Dehydrated Dog Treats

Dehydrated dog treats are a fantastic way to provide your furry friend with healthy, nutritious snacks without additives and preservatives usually found in store-bought options. Using a dehydrator, you can easily create a variety of tasty treats that are economical and tailored to your dog's specific tastes and dietary needs. This guide will walk you through the basics of making dehydrated dog treats, offering simple recipes and tips to ensure your homemade snacks are a hit with your canine companion.

Chicken Jerky: Cut chicken breasts into thin strips. Dehydrate at 145°F (63°C) for 8-10 hours until completely dry and crisp.

Apple Rings: Core and slice apples into 1/4-inch rings. Dehydrate at 135°F (57°C) for 6-8 hours until dry and leathery.

Carrot Chips: Slice carrots into thin rounds or strips. Dehydrate at 135°F (57°C) for 6-8 hours until crisp.

Banana Bites: Slice bananas into 1/4-inch rounds. Dehydrate at 135°F (57°C) for 6-8 hours until leathery.

Beef Liver Treats: Slice beef liver into thin strips. Dehydrate at 145°F (63°C) for 10-12 hours until completely dry.

Pumpkin Slices: Cut pumpkin into 1/4-inch slices. Dehydrate at 135°F (57°C) for 6-8 hours until dry and firm.

Green Bean Crunchies: Trim the ends off the green beans and cut them in half. Dehydrate at 135°F (57°C) for 6-8 hours until crisp.

Pear Slices: Core and slice pears into 1/4-inch rings. Dehydrate at 135°F (57°C) for 6-8 hours until dry and leathery.

Zucchini Chips: Slice zucchini into thin rounds. Dehydrate at 135°F (57°C) for 6-8 hours until crisp.

- Ensure all pieces are of uniform thickness for even drying.

- Store dehydrated snacks in airtight containers in a cool, dry place.

From sweet potato chews and chicken jerky to apple rings and carrot chips, these recipes are easy to follow and perfect for beginners. The possibilities are virtually endless. Dehydrating treats lets you control the ingredients and ensure your dog enjoys healthy, natural snacks. Remember to slice ingredients uniformly for even drying, store treats properly, and always supervise your dog when trying new treats. With these recipes, you can confidently provide delicious and wholesome snacks your dog will love.

And, oddly enough, you might find yourself enjoying these unusual treats!

Training Rewards

Treats should only make up a small portion of your dog's diet. Overall, homemade treats are a way for people to show their dogs how much they care. They're a way to make training fun and rewarding and help keep dogs healthy, and crunchy treats are a great way to maintain oral hygiene! And, of course, you aren't running to pull something from a bag or box with unknown nutritional benefits. You know precisely what your dog is getting when giving homemade treats.

When training our wiggle-butts, patience and persistence are key. And what better way to motivate them than with homemade treats? These treats are more than bribes; they serve as clear signs of approval, helping guide our pups through commands and behaviors. It's essential to make sure these treats are high-quality, given with intention, and used in moderation. This positive reinforcement method keeps dogs engaged, motivated, and eager to learn. With the proper treats, training becomes a fun game of celebrating successes!

Caution… treats for training doesn't mean a treat for every action. Repeating a training exercise twenty times should not warrant twenty treats! Overdoing treats is like overdoing any food item; while the puppies love it, it may not be great for their weight.

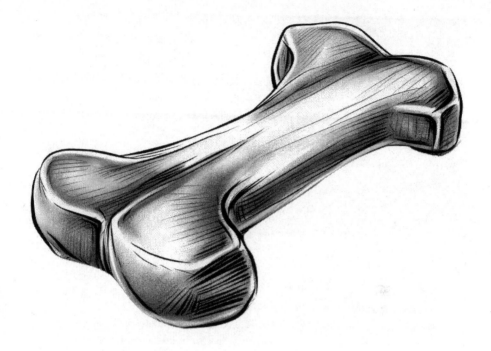

11.7.1 Dehydrated Sweet Potato Chews

Dehydrated Sweet Potato Chews offer a simple, healthy, and delicious treat option for dogs of all sizes. Sweet potatoes are a fantastic source of grain-free dietary fiber, aiding digestive health. Sweet potatoes contain beta-carotene, which converts to Vitamin A in the body to support eye health and immune function. By dehydrating the sweet potatoes, you concentrate their natural sugars for a hint of sweetness that dogs love without adding artificial flavors or preservatives. This nutritious homemade treat provides a satisfying chewy texture that can help support dental health by cleaning teeth and strengthening gums as your dog chews. Perfect for pets with food sensitivities or those on a limited-ingredient diet, these chews are a wholesome, easy-to-make snack your dog will surely enjoy.

DEHYDRATED
SWEET POTATO CHEWS

 CAL / SERVING: 35

 PROTEIN: 1 g

 CARBOHYDRATES: 8 g

 FAT: 1 g

 FIBER: 1 g

 SERVINGS: 20

INGREDIENTS

☐ 2 large sweet potatoes *(rich in beta-carotene, vitamins, and fiber)*

Cooling: Let sweet potato chews cool completely before storing them in an airtight container.

Storage: Keep in a cool, dry place for up to 3 weeks. Refrigerate for longer storage, up to 3 months.

Air Fry: If you don't have a dehydrator, use an air fryer, set to 180°F if possible; depending on thickness, you should get some decent treats in about 3 - 4 hours.

DIRECTIONS

Prep the Sweet Potatoes:

Wash sweet potatoes thoroughly. Peeling is optional; leaving the skin on adds nutrients and fiber.

Slice sweet potatoes into 1/4-inch slices for faster drying or 1/2-inch for chewier treats.

Oven Method:

Preheat oven to the lowest setting, ideally around 175°F (80C). Place slices on a baking sheet lined with parchment paper, ensuring they're not touching for even dehydration. Bake for 6-8 hours, flipping halfway. Time varies based on thickness; aim for chewiness, not crispness.

Dehydrator Method:

Arrange slices on dehydrator trays. Set the dehydrator to 125°F (52°C) and run for 8 - 10 hours, checking for desired texture.

CHEF'S TIP

Chapter 12:

OTHER STRATEGIES FOR YOUR DOG'S DIET

A few things to begin. Broad thoughts on diet.

1. I have been researching and joining many Facebook groups on dogs and dog food to learn more about the target audience and gather ideas for this book. Many people like sharing pictures of their homemade dog food in these groups. However, they often receive criticism for not including diverse ingredients in their meals. It's important to note that just because certain nutrients aren't visible in the food doesn't mean they're not present. For example, omega-3 fatty acids, essential for a dog's skin and coat health, might not be apparent in the food but are still beneficial for your dog's health.

My dogs enjoy a variety of foods, from braised turkey necks to beef and chicken bones and canned salmon, which they can snack on between meals. I want to stress the importance of a diverse diet for dogs, as it allows us to balance their nutritional needs with various ingredients. By avoiding feeding your dog the same homemade food daily, you're taking a responsible step towards their health. I also include a multivitamin and probiotic supplement in Dot's meals every other day to ensure she doesn't develop any unforeseen nutrient deficiencies.

So, let's avoid jumping on others trying to make homemade food for their dogs. Let us support what they are doing, even if it isn't perfect the first time.

2. Our intention is not to demonize kibble-type foods. They do have a place in the overall picture of the canine diet. It's a cheap and affordable way to supplement your dog's diet with crucial nutrients that may be hard to find in traditional ingredients, so as long as we adhere to our concept of 'not feeding your dog the same thing every day,' having kibble here and there is okay, it can help with nutrient deficiencies, and due to the crunchy nature of the kibble and treats, they help with dental hygiene.

3. And remember, since I might not have mentioned it so far, it almost goes without saying: Making homemade dog food guarantees your vet bills will be lower overall. Yes, you will spend more for initial consults and hopefully not too much on kitchen gear, but as your dog gets healthier and has fewer problems, you will see the vet less and spend less on that part of your doggie's upkeep.

12.1 Smart Shopping: Quality Ingredients for Less

Have you ever been to a bustling market early in the morning where vendors are setting up their stalls and the air is full of the promise of fresh produce and great deals? A market is the perfect setting for a discussion on how to shop smartly for pet food that is both healthy and affordable. The quality of our chosen ingredients directly impacts our dog's health and our budget's sustainability. While finding good quality pet food at a reasonable price may seem challenging, it's not impossible. With some know-how, strategy, and an open mind, we can make food choices that benefit our pets, the environment, and communities. By shopping smartly and seeking high-quality ingredients at lower costs, we can positively engage with the food system and help our pets stay healthy and happy.

When we talk about the market, there are a few things to consider wherever you are and whatever time of year. Markets have/get large amounts of produce daily. Not all of it is 'pretty' for the display, so this product is often put in the back, so to speak, or not displayed at all. Pick up this 'scratch and dent' product for half or less of the regular price. It is still okay for eating, cooking, and doggie use, but it's not very pretty. And saving half or more of your budget for fruits and vegetables… is a huge consideration.

Similarly, at the end of market day, unless it is a seven-day-a-week market, the owner will have a few leftovers s/he doesn't want to return to the farm/house/ storage. Same deal: take it all for half, use it in your recipes one way or another, and cut your bill by a significant number weekly, year after year. After a while, the same people will know you will come around for the dented or the end-of-day produce and may offer you a 'bag' deal as in a bulk discount.

If you don't get a positive response at one market, go to another. Eventually, you will establish yourself in a market and be able to take advantage of these deals. Ask your friends around who also haunt markets. They will know who is flexible and who isn't.

Seasonal Purchases

The rhythm of the seasons dictates not just the weather but also the bounty available in our markets. Fruits and vegetables picked at the peak of their ripeness boast superior flavor and higher nutritional content, offering a feast for the senses and a boon for health. This abundance typically translates to lower prices as the market adjusts to the surplus. Shopping by season becomes a dual act of nourishment and economy, ensuring our dogs enjoy the freshest meals without straining our finances.

Imagine a crisp autumn morning, the market stalls laden with the vibrant oranges of pumpkins and the deep kale greens—a visual and nutritional harvest ripe for the taking. Incorporating these into your dog's diet capitalizes on seasonal nutrients. It aligns your shopping habits with the Earth's natural cycles, fostering a connection to the environment that sustains us.

Also, if you are dehydrating or freezing produce, seasonal buying is a great way to buy in bulk and get even better prices. More on buying in bulk is below.

Wholesale Clubs and Discounts

Did you know that joining wholesale clubs can help you save a lot of money on feeding your dog a homemade diet? These clubs offer discounts on buying meat and vegetables in bulk, which can help you get high-quality ingredients at lower prices than traditional stores.

This strategy is similar to how chefs in restaurants buy their ingredients in bulk to save money without sacrificing the quality of their dishes. However, this approach requires you to invest in a membership and storage to keep the ingredients fresh. But, it's worth it in the long run as you can offer your furry friends a delicious and healthy meal without breaking the bank.

Also, remember to compare prices across different stores or online platforms to find the best deals on high-quality ingredients for your dog's meals. This will ensure that every meal you serve is healthy and cost-effective.

Buy in Bulk

Buying in bulk can reduce costs without sacrificing the quality of staples like rice and certain vegetables. This practice, common among those who prepare for long winters or manage large households, relies on the simple economy of scale principle—the more you buy, the less you pay per unit.

Imagine stocking a pantry in anticipation of a busy season, filling shelves with jars of grains and bins of root vegetables, and ensuring the hearth and home are ready for the months ahead. This foresight, applied to shopping for ingredients for homemade dog food, not only provides a ready supply of essential items but also minimizes the frequency of shopping trips, saving time and money.

When purchasing items in large quantities, create a list of all the ingredients used in your dog's meals. Then, note which items can be stored, dehydrated, frozen, or refrigerated for more extended periods. Many of these ingredients have specific times of the year when they are most affordable. For example, corn is often best bought from July to October, and other fruits and vegetables also have optimal purchasing times. Additionally, staples like rice, grains, and potatoes also have optimal times for purchase, some due to harvesting seasons and others due to sales at grocery stores. For example, sweet potatoes, pumpkins, whole turkeys, and yams are often discounted before Thanksgiving, while cabbage is on sale in mid-March for St. Patrick's Day corned beef and cabbage dishes.

12.2 Growing Your Ingredients: A Garden for You and Your Dog

Starting Small

Starting a garden that provides fresh and healthy food for humans and dogs doesn't need to be complicated. You can begin with a small area or just a few containers and choose vegetables and herbs that are easy to grow and nutritious. Lettuce is a great place to start because it grows fast and can be a crunchy treat for dogs when used in moderation. Carrots are another excellent choice as they offer sweet roots for humans to eat and nutritious tops for dogs to enjoy.

Dog-Safe Plants

When creating a garden, it's essential to be vigilant and choose plants that won't harm our dog's health. Some herbs, like parsley and rosemary, are suitable for cooking and great for dogs as they freshen their breath and improve their circulation. Blueberries are also a good choice, as they are tasty and full of antioxidants that benefit dogs and their owners.

Note that planting tomatoes is dangerous. The tomatoes are fine, but the stalk and leaves are toxic to animals and humans. It is important for you to check on every plant you are planting to ensure it is safe for BOTH humans and animals, specifically dogs, as some potentially harmful plants are not a problem for other animals with different digestive systems. It takes a bit of work but is a requirement if you plan to have the garden anywhere the dogs, children, and you can get to it. By carefully selecting dog-friendly plants, the garden will be a safe and enjoyable place for all, where every harvest is a delight.

Composting

Composting is a fantastic way to recycle waste in a garden and make it functional. Instead of throwing away food scraps and eggshells, collect them in a bin. The scraps can break down naturally into super-rich soil, perfect for growing healthy fruits and veggies that feed people and animals. Composting is fantastic because it helps reduce waste and makes the garden stronger and more nutritious. Make sure to keep it in a place where animals, children, and visitors cannot access it.

12.3 Community Resources: Bulk Buying and Food Shares

In our local communities, there are many ways to get food for our dogs beyond just buying it at a store. We can work with others in our community to share resources and ensure our dogs are well-fed, affordably, and sustainably. From community food co-ops to trading systems, we can find ways to provide our fur babies with high-quality food without breaking the bank. It's all about working together and being mindful of how we can care for our pets in a way that benefits everyone.

Food Co-ops and Buying Clubs

Food cooperatives and buying clubs unite individuals to pursue bulk goods at reduced rates. By pooling resources, members gain leverage, enabling access to premium ingredients at a fraction of the cost—akin to a collective bargaining power that benefits each participant. In the communal effort to procure, there lies a shared commitment to the well-being of all members' canine companions, ensuring each has access to the nourishment they deserve. Many communities call these farm truck clubs because a farmer agrees to deliver certain fruits and vegetables weekly from spring to fall for a specific seasonal price. This agreement gives the farmer a guaranteed source of income and sales for his crops and allows the members to get fresh food every week. Usually, the food is bagged or boxed and delivered to a familiar drop-off spot. Don't expect door-to-door service here, but the prices will be solid, and the service will as well.

Farmers' Markets & Bartering

Building relationships with local market farmers is a great way to get our dogs fresh, healthy produce and meats. These connections can lead to better deals and information about upcoming harvests, which can help us plan our dogs' meals more efficiently. By conversing with growers, we can learn more about where our food comes from and how it's grown. This ties in with finding some vendors at the market and making scratch-and-dent and end-of-day deals with them.

Additionally, we can use bartering, an ancient system of exchanging goods or services without money, to get high-quality ingredients for our dogs' food. For example, we can trade our homegrown vegetables for cuts of meat or surplus eggs. This system fosters a sense of community and values exchange over acquisition, ensuring everyone benefits from their contributions. You only need to ask what the farmer/marketeer needs in exchange and arrange to exchange it. If you happen to have, for example, acres and acres of Persian Mint (an inside joke for those growing it), it is valuable to trade. If you are in the crate, box, or bag business,... also things the farmers will need for market days and deliveries. Think outside the box and ask around... you will be surprised at how you can make a deal and keep your doggie feeding costs down.

Community Gardens

Community gardens are great places to plant and grow fruits and vegetables. Dog owners participating in these gardens can provide fresh produce to supplement their pets' diets.

By participating in community resources like co-ops and gardens, dog owners can help support local economies and contribute to the principles of sustainability and mutual support. This journey highlights the power of working together and sharing resources. It can deepen people's connection to their communities and the natural world.

Overall, I want to encourage dog owners to explore new ways of providing healthy and nutritious food for their pets while engaging with and contributing to their communities.

12.4 Keeping the Game Alive

Now you have everything you need to create mouthwatering, nutrient-packed homemade meals for your dog, and it's time to pass on your newfound knowledge and show other readers where they can get the same help.

Leaving your honest opinion of this book on Amazon will show other dog owners where they can find the information they're looking for and share your passion for your fur babies.

Thank you for being so helpful. The joy of homemade dog food stays alive when we pass on our knowledge, and you're helping me to do just that.

In addition to leaving reviews, do the 'one better' thing. Buy a copy of the book for your other dog-loving friends and family. There is always a reason or excuse to give a gift, and this one could be a lifesaver for a dog or a family member.

Scan the QR code below to leave your review:

CONCLUSION

As we draw the curtains on this culinary 'Tail' through the world of homemade dog nutrition, reflecting on the ground we've covered together is incredible. From those first steps to understanding the bedrock of canine nutritional needs to mastering the art of meal planning and preparation, we've navigated a transformative path. It's been a ride full of discovery, debunking myths, and embracing the future of canine wellbeing.

Reflecting on my personal story with Dot, it's clear how our journey into homemade dog food reshaped my perspective on pet care. Cooking for Dot was more than just preparing meals—it was a language of love, a testament to our profound connection. I hope through these pages, you've felt inspired to explore that same bond with your dog.

Throughout this book, we've tackled the essentials of crafting a nutritious diet, the empowerment of taking charge of your dog's health, and the importance of continuous learning and community involvement. By equipping you with the tools and confidence needed, I hope to have ignited a passion for canine culinary arts that goes beyond the bowl.

Now, I encourage you to take that first step, armed with a spatula and love, to start cooking for your dog. Even the most straightforward recipes can mark the beginning of an incredible transformation in their health, vitality, and the bond you share. Witness firsthand the joy from a wagging tail and eager eyes at mealtime.

I am deeply grateful for your joining me on this flavorful journey. Your openness to embracing the joy and satisfaction of cooking for your fur babies fills me with hope. Together, let's envision a future where more pets thrive on nutritious, homemade meals, supported by a vibrant community of pet owners sharing their triumphs and challenges.

As we part ways, remember the journey doesn't end here. Let this be the first step into a world where every meal celebrates health and love. Here's to a future brimming with happy, healthy dogs nourished by the hands of those who love them most. Cheers to many joyful meals ahead and the enduring bonds they forge.

Thank you, from the bottom of my heart and Dot's, too, for embarking on this culinary adventure with us.

REFERENCES

1. Canine Works. (2018, March 5). *Fish for dogs: Which to avoid and which to feed*. https://canineworks.com.au/health-articles/2018/3/5/fish-for-dogs-which-to-avoid-and-which-to-feed

2. PetMD. (n.d.). *AAFCO-approved pet food: Everything you need to know*. https://www.petmd.com/dog/nutrition/What-Is-AAFCO-and-What-Does-It-Do

3. JustFoodForDogs. (n.d.). *Nutritionally complete homemade dog food recipes*. https://www.justfoodfordogs.com/blog/nutritionally-complete-homemade-dog-food-recipes.html

4. The Wildest. (n.d.). *22 important vitamins and minerals for your dog*. https://www.thewildest.com/dog-nutrition/important-vitamins-and-minerals-your-dog

5. American Kennel Club. (n.d.). *Homemade dog food recipes: Choosing balanced ingredients*. https://www.akc.org/expert-advice/nutrition/choosing-ingredients-homemade-dog-food/

6. American Kennel Club. (n.d.). *Food allergies in dogs: What to know*. https://www.akc.org/expert-advice/health/dog-food-allergies/

7. Wag Tantrum. (n.d.). *The benefits of organic fresh dog food for your pup*. https://wagtantrum.com/blogs/news/the-benefits-of-organic-dog-food-for-your-pup

8. Loona Well. (n.d.). *How to preserve dog food without synthetic preservatives*. https://www.loonawell.com/a/blog/how-to-preserve-dog-food-without-synthetic-preservatives

9. Hearthstone Homemade Dog Food. (n.d.). *Getting started with homemade dog food*. https://www.hearthstonehomemadedogfood.com/getting-started-with-diy-dog-food

10. Ware, M. (2020, January 24). *How cooking affects the nutrient content of foods*. Healthline. https://www.healthline.com/nutrition/cooking-

nutrient-content

11. Dogster. (n.d.). *How to store homemade dog food: 6 vet-reviewed tips*. https://www.dogster.com/dog-nutrition/how-to-store-homemade-dog-food

12. Healthy Paws Pet Insurance. (n.d.). *How to make vet-approved homemade dog food*. https://blog.healthypawspetinsurance.com/make-vet-approved-homemade-dog-food

13. iHeartDogs. (n.d.). *7 best homemade dog food supplements*. https://iheartdogs.com/best-homemade-dog-food-supplements/#:~:text=Essential%20supplements%20for%20a%20homemade%20dog%20diet%20typically%20include%20vitamins,E%2C%20to%20support%20overall%20wellbeing.

14. A Fork's Tale. (n.d.). *Easy homemade dog food crockpot recipe with ground beef*. https://www.aforkstale.com/easy-homemade-crockpot-dog-food/

15. The Wildest. (n.d.). *How to calculate and track calories in your dog*. https://www.thewildest.com/dog-nutrition/dog-calorie-calculation-advice

16. Union Lake Veterinary Hospital. (n.d.). *A beginner's guide to home cooking for dogs*. https://unionlakeveterinaryhospital.com/blog/a-beginners-guide-to-home-cooking-for-dogs

17. Vetericyn. (n.d.). *Signs and symptoms of dog nutritional deficiencies*. https://vetericyn.com/blog/signs-and-symptoms-of-dog-nutritional-deficiencies/

18. PetMD. (n.d.). *How many calories does a dog need?* https://www.petmd.com/dog/nutrition/how-many-calories-does-a-dog-need

19. PAWSM. (n.d.). *PAWSM – Dog nutrition mobile application*. https://pawsm.com/

20. ToeGrips. (n.d.). *Find your dog's body condition score (BCS)*. https://toegrips.com/canine-body-condition-score/

21. DVM 360. (2022, October 14). *Canine nutrition study results support plant-based diet*. https://www.dvm360.com/view/canine-nutrition-study-results-support-plant-based-diet

22. The Wildest. (n.d.). *Save money with homemade dog food*. https://www.thewildest.com/dog-nutrition/save-money-homemade-dog-food

23. NetMeds. (2022, October 20). *Personalized pet nutrition: Uses, benefits, and ways to optimize health*. https://www.netmeds.com/health-library/post/personalized-nutrition-for-pets-uses-benefits-and-ways-to-optimize-health

24. PubMed. (2017, June). *Functional foods in pet nutrition: Focus on dogs and cats*. https://pubmed.ncbi.nlm.nih.gov/28433933/

25. Global Pet Industry. (n.d.). *Technology and pet food quality*. https://globalpetindustry.com/article/technology-and-pet-food-quality

26. Dog Food Advisor. (n.d.). *How to choose a sustainable dog food*. https://www.dogfoodadvisor.com/choosing-dog-food/choosing-sustainable-dog-food/

27. Jangada Sea. (n.d.). *Choosing the best dog food for different breeds*. https://jangadasea.com/choosing-the-best-dog-food-for-different-breeds/

28. RawFedK9. (n.d.). *Dog feeding guidelines for raw food*. https://rawfedk9.com/blogs/news/dog-feeding-guidelines-for-raw-food

29. Centers for Disease Control and Prevention. (n.d.). *Pet food safety | Healthy pets, healthy people*. https://www.cdc.gov/healthypets/keeping-pets-and-people-healthy/pet-food-safety.html

30. Dr. Ruth Roberts. (n.d.). *Seasonal eating: A year-round diet to keep your pet healthy*. https://drruthroberts.com/blogs/pet-blog/seasonal-eating-a-year-round-diet-to-keep-your-pet-healthy#:~:text=Nutritional%20Quality%3A%20Seasonal%20produce%20is,to%20their%20off%2Dseason%20counterparts.

Kitchen Conversions

MEASUREMENTS

CUPS	OUNCES	MILLILTERS	TBSP
8	64	1892.7	128
6	48	1419.5	96
5	40	1182.9	80
4	32	946.4	64
2	16	480	32
1	8	236.6	16
3/4	6	177	12
2/3	5	157.6	10Tbsp + 2 tsp
1/2	4	118	8
3/8	3	90	6
1/3	2.5	80	5 Tbsp + 1 tsp
1/4	2	59	4
1/8	1	30	3
1/16	1/2	15	1

TEMPERATURE

FARENHEIT	CELCIUS
100	37
150	65
200	93
250	121
300	149
325	163.5
350	176.7
375	190
400	204
425	219
450	232
500	260
525	274
550	288

REDUCTIONS

CUPS	HALF	1/3
1	1/2 cup	1/3 cup
3/4	6 Tbsp	1/4 cup
2/3	1/3 Cup	3 Tbsp+ 1-1/2 tsp
1/2	1/4 cup	2 Tbsp +2 tsp
1/3	2 Tbsp + 2 tsp	1 Tbsp + 1/4 tsp
1/4	2 Tbsp	1 Tbsp + tsp
1 Tbsp	1-1/2 tsp	1 tsp
1 tsp	1/2 tsp	1/4 tsp
1/2 tsp	1/4 tsp	1/8 tsp
1/4 tsp	1/8 tsp	dash

MOST USED

1 Cup	1/2 pint
2 Cups	1 pint
4 Cups	1 quart
2 pints	1 quart
4 quarts	1 Gallon
3 tsp	1 Tbsp
4 Tbsp	1/4 cups
8 Tbsp	1/2 cup

WEIGHT

IMPERIAL	METRIC
1/2 oz	15 g
1 oz	29 g
2 oz	57 g
3 oz	85 g
4 oz	113 g
5 oz	141 g
6 oz	170 g
8 oz	227 g
10 oz	283 g
12 oz	340 g
13 oz	369 g
14 oz	397 g
15 oz	425 g
1 lb	453 g

Made in the USA
Columbia, SC
10 December 2024

48939401R00087